SIDDHANTA YOGA A

INVOKING REALITY

THE SPONTANEOUS TEACHINGS OF
JIVANMUKTI

ON THE ESSENCE OF SIDDHA KUNDALINI YOGA
&
SPIRITUAL AWAKENING

EDITED BY J. HENRY, P. WALTERS, C. EDWARD

Published by Siddhanta Yoga Academy, 2021

Copyright © Jivanmukti & Siddhanta Yoga Academy, 2021

Compiled and edited by J. Henry, P. Walters, C. Edward

Cover design by Jivanmukti

ISBN: 9798598029299

This book is a record of the Spontaneous Teachings of Jivanmukti (comprised of Jivanmukti's correspondence with spiritual seekers), which emanate Higher Knowledge and Wisdom embodied and transmitted through Jivanmukti's presence. Jivanmukti's words carry in them an immense spiritual power to return one to the natural flow of life, to invoke the living spiritual teaching within and to dispel illusions on the path of awakening and self-refinement. Beyond the words themselves, the book is the flow of spiritual transmission, which instantly reconnects the reader to the very essence of the natural Being – The Ultimate Reality. Any such moment of reconnection can become a moment of a profound shift or inner awakening. Any genuine spiritual seeker will benefit greatly from this inspiring Book and the rare spiritual gems that it contains.

ACKNOWLEDGEMENTS

This work would not have been possible without the contribution of Jivanmukti's followers and spiritual seekers who instigated these enlightening dialogues and made this invaluable book of spiritual enquiry possible. This work would not have been accomplished without the dedicated efforts of Jivanmukti's adepts in compiling and editing.

CONTENTS

FOREWORD

This book is a testimony to the reality of spiritual evolution in the human body. It is a guide for those facing the inner, self-inflicted limitations that blind us from seeing the real path of evolution. It illustrates how the multiplicity of present-day pseudo-spirituality and life can be dissolved into the simplicity of Self-Being, and invoked within as the unavoidable Reality of human existence as an aware awakened being, by refining and eventually integrating the self within the natural blissful Being of the Ultimate Reality.

One of the most important threads running through the questions and answers of this book is disillusionment. Spiritual disillusionment occurs when knowledge that is second-hand or merely speculative meets the genuine, vibrant-in-its core self-born knowledge – the very essence of our Conscious existence, the very Being beyond the projected world and all sorts of illusions – the Ultimate Reality. Such Knowledge is pure transmission devoid of concepts, ideas, thoughts or emotional patterns, and is thus free from the corruption of one's individual perception and can be experienced through the absorption of one's individual consciousness into the natural, unconditional space of existence.

The Direct Transmission of self-born knowledge is more like an emanation than a voluntary intention, and it has the ability to shift one's consciousness and invoke the experience of the Unconditional Reality within the one who receives it. Thus, spiritual guidance and communication between the adept and the teacher is a constant dance of sharing and transmission. As the adept shares their sincere questions with the vessel of self-born knowledge (the teacher), the teacher responds in a way that both reflects the limitations within the space of their questioning-consciousness, and invokes the experience of the Ultimate Reality, which is beyond any limited conditional perspective. In such a Reality, there is neither adept nor teacher but simply the Knowledge of existence itself, which contains all within the eternal Awareness.

When Spiritual Knowledge is shared, it is done so by the effortless and pure emanation of one's Natural Being. There is no imposition. It is like standing in the rays of the sun. If one stays in them for too long or at the wrong time, one gets burnt. In the same manner does one evolve through one's interaction with the existence within the Self. Self-refinement is a process of dissolving one's obscured self-perception by the constant letting go of the previous moment within the self, which leads to the process of integrating the radiation of the Ultimate with the limited, through the individual vessel of consciousness.

The idea of spiritual questioning and enquiry in general, is to arrive at the point of questionlessness. When one abides in the blissful empty Being, there is no question of anything. There may remain a childlike curiosity about various aspects of creation and manifestation, but those questions that seek an ultimate answer in order to somehow settle and box the mysterious experience and essence of life, can only be answered by the silence itself, the bliss, and the potent, all-encompassing emptiness of the Ultimate Wholesome and Unconditional Existence.

Thus, it is the Conscious Reality itself that answers questions of a spiritual nature. Within that pointless point of emptiness and infinite non-knowing, everything objective, finite and conditioned can be known and seen for what it is. The very point of interacting with a qualified spiritual teacher is to gradually dissolve one's limitations into their greater, or rather, more integrated space of awareness.

The evolutionary link between an adept and a teacher exists within the space of Consciousness itself, which imbibes the very connection, is the reason for it and is its nourishment. Yet, the separation between an adept and a teacher is illusionary. Through the meditative absorption, all the notions of adept and teacher, teaching and learning, knowing and not knowing dissolve into the single space of the unconditional Being, the Consciousness itself. That very Consciousness that abides all, at the same time appears as the teacher and the adept in the physical reality, and by the reflection and through the interaction, initiates the very process of teaching and learning as if through two different vessels.

The true link between the teacher and the student is imperceivable by others yet is always there nurturing and empowering. Such a connection is far from being limited to verbal exchanges or outwardly obvious displays of teaching or wise words. The very presence and the words of the teacher are impregnated with the very reality and Conscious emanation of intelligent existence. Such a connection is one that if consciously and sincerely nurtured and selflessly unfolded within, becomes a powerful spiritual emanation and an invisible field of transmission of the unconditional Presence and Knowledge – the vortex of teaching and learning – the living lineage of Siddha Param-Para.

Through the power of transmission, one is able to connect to the very space of teaching and learning and to discover this unconditional space within the self. Through the link between a living teacher and an adept, one is able to deepen one's awareness and connection with the projected and subtler realities by dissolving the logical ways of understanding the transitory realities and waves of existence, to gradually dissolve them within the self and to realise the essence of the Ultimate Being that abides everything and *is* the unified existence. By merging into the same space of Consciousness with the teacher and by refining the self through that space, one realises the Reality of the Self beyond names, forms, titles and any forms of conditioning.

By the spontaneous recognition and reconnection with that Reality through the Living Teaching, all of one's limited spiritual notions, ideas and misconceptions dissolve into the unified space of existence and the spontaneous and effortless realisation of one's being, and the essence of all the spiritual sciences and teachings begin to emerge in the very space of embodied consciousness. Thus, one's true spiritual journey begins.

It is often through a word, a question or a simple exchange that the path to the true spiritual reality is initiated. Yet, the path itself is made up of thousands of such spontaneous exchanges of a self-refining nature, which make the teaching and learning process 'living', invigorating and yet unpredictable, and that make it possible for dedicated adepts to eventually break through all sorts of conditionings and limitations, to realise and to establish the self in the Ultimate. It is from many of these spontaneous exchanges that this book began. And so, your spiritual journey may begin too.

PREFACE

Invoking Reality means coming back to the natural flow of Being, which is always there – the Reality that exists beyond the man-made reality and the corruption of the current age. Current spirituality appears to be so forced, so unnatural and limited. We feel a compulsion towards spiritual action because we do not perceive the internal link with creation, which abides all and connects everything within the existence. That is why, we are currently living in the era of degradation. This degradation and corruption means that we are not within the natural flow of creation and existence, but rather, exist within the limitations that we have imposed on ourselves. In past, more balanced ages, people would not need to make journeys, be a part of anything, or perform any actions in order to become anything. They were already connected with the natural flow of existence, which ran through their being, through their veins. They did not need to create taboos, divide life in any way or please supernatural forces. They were a part of the natural world, part of a reality that has been long since forgotten.

It is wisdom to perceive life and understand its currents. Without realising the dynamics of life currents, life is a random happening, where everyone becomes a part of the endless emotional and mental stimulation and manipulation. If one is to be a spiritual adept, one is to have courage to admit one's own weaknesses to oneself and to live by aspiring towards the dissolution of such weaknesses within the self, by abstaining from unconscious actions or actions driven by blind emotions. One should only act when there is flow from within. True flow is equanimous and selfless and imbues wisdom and deep spiritual universal intelligence and purity. In such a flow, there is only Expression, free from after-thoughts of control, attachment and possessiveness. Such a flow is a beautiful Being of the Ultimate and is hard to spot through the mundane reality. That is why we feel that we need to go through some sort of process of awakening – simply to come back to the flow and acknowledge it within ourselves. Only through this acknowledgment can we return to the natural and perceive the eternal.

Through this natural flow, even when it is perceived only as feeble at the start, we initiate the process of refinement. This opens up a stronger inner current of being within ourselves which eventually expands to a greater natural flow – from a feeble, almost unnoticeable stream, to a flow of life that abides all and contains all. Yet, it is so subtle that it can only be known in those who consciously acknowledged it and return to it, fully immersing oneself in it, refining through it, and bathing in it unconditionally. Such beings are known as true and rare spiritual Adepts, those who have realised the stream within and expanded it into the greater flow of existence.

They who became that flow and realised that nothing within the self is separate from the flow, are the greatest of the beings on Earth. They dissolved all that which is unreal, which draws attention to the separate elements and invokes false perceptions of superiority and the importance of one element over the other, draining such being from within, blinding one from seeing the flow of Being that abides all and that flows through all the elements equally. To restore such an equal perception of the flow is already a great first step, which lays the foundation for the dissolution of impurities within the field of self-perception and the perception of Reality. This process cannot be forced, practiced, or even noticed before the point of inner maturity. And it is but a natural flow of evolution where one's being dissolves perceptual veils and dives consciously into the ever-flowing eternal stream of life.

There is beauty in errors and pleasures; both draw the conscious mature mind into the stream of eternal life. Only immature minds complain and do not see the beauty of such a dynamic. They divide life and attach to one of the extremes or wonder unconsciously. They thus drain themselves immaturely, blinded, deaf and unaware of the eternal current (stream, flow) within the self. The beauty of life is there to either turn us within or to enslave us. The choice depends on the maturity of the being and one's ability to recognise the opportunity to return to the natural eternal flow by embracing the external flow of life and dissolving it within without separating it into two opposites. Only mature and selfless beings are able to recognise and to realise it. All the rest pursue one current over the other, ignorantly splitting the flow into two. That is why they cannot know the Existence of the Ultimate Being beyond such a division, and why they keep on deluding themselves, walking in circles and searching for something within the scope of their veiled perception, ignoring that which is always there. Failing to recognise it, they are thus unable to return to it. Such people waste their lives on foolish pursuits and believe in all sorts of nonsense driven by the limited currents or veils of perception. They search for the eternal in the transitory, and thus never find it. They become the slaves of their own illusions.

Maturity is the quality of an adept. It cannot be bought or seen from the outside. One can be recognised as a mature being only by those who are able to see subtler levels of the embodied being. That is why no one can truly know who is who, unless they first know themselves, and why one is only able to penetrate, with their awareness, as deeply as they are able to perceive themselves within the current of life. As long as one is swimming and struggling with external resistance to the one natural current, they will be unable to see or recognise others for their maturity. Only when the external currents subside into the natural smooth equanimous flow of life, and one becomes that flow, does one attain the clarity of the pure sky and see all phenomena as they are at their core. Then, one is able to recognise the maturity of the soul beyond judgment and external veils.

The True flow of life is incorruptible. The corruption exists within individual experiences and the individual interpretation only. When experience is seen as experience, and the Eternal Flow of life is perceived at all times as the Ultimate Self-Being, no experience drains, attaches or deludes, but only dissolves as fast as it arises in one's conscious flow. Every experience arises and subsides within the eternal now, like a wave rising and subsiding without being remembered. Such is the space of Consciousness. It is always pure no matter how many waves arise on it. They subside into the same space and leave no trace. Only an observer may say that something has happened. But who is there to observe?

Thus, Eternity is imperceivable. It just is.

THE ESSENCE OF JIVANMUKTI'S TEACHING THROUGH SHAKTIPAT STREAM

Many wonder about the way spiritual teaching and learning happens. Many look for words and many stumble at various forms of occult knowledge, rituals and overall action-driven spirituality. In this day and age, it is but impossible to come across something genuine or true or to even know the standard of that which is pure and genuine. True spirituality is a natural in-and-out flow of our individual being or soul, which emanates a certain frequency and attracts an experience to it through this very frequency. If we understand this simple mechanism, we can realise that true spirituality is not something that you simply come across but is the very outcome of your internal being which looks for answers, experiences, and knowledge (most of the time, in the ways it perceives the reality from within).

When it comes to natural spirituality, nothing can or should be forced or imposed. Natural Spirituality means that it is emanating and connecting, through the same resonance, with a mature being (soul). Spiritual Knowledge is often misinterpreted and is seen as something that one almost tangibly acquires. Yet, true spiritual knowledge is a frequency that can be perceived once one is able to invoke it within the self and maintain it through natural meditative absorption. If one asks whether there is a method of acquiring true spiritual knowledge, the answer would be, yes, there is one and the only method – direct transmission. Yet, this method should not be confused with the transmission received from other beings.

In this world, through this reality, we are constantly in the mode of receiving and giving transmissions, yet these transmissions are of various frequencies and resonances, and very often, are impure or polluted by the field of chaotic emotions and thoughts. True spiritual transmission is a different type of frequency and field, which cannot be experienced just through one's desire. It is so much more than mere theoretical knowledge. It is first of all, Knowledge (experience, being) that cannot be described or compared to anything we know of within the Reality of tangible thoughts and emotions. Thus, in order to experience this reality of knowledge, one is to have such qualities invoked within oneself, so that these qualities or waves of emanation of one's being, would clear the path of knowledge reception and the ability to contain it within the self.

Even though we are trying to put this experience of knowledge into words, find a logical explanation for it and frame it into a method, it has never been or will be a method. This is why it is called a 'way' or a 'path of being' – because it is a path of presence and emanation, direct experience and being a vessel of that experience, not just empty words. Such forms of knowledge are subtle and so far, evolutionarily advanced. They cannot be understood by any contemporary average being who is engrossed in the reality of tangible thoughts and emotions. This knowledge is invoked through the power of spiritual absorption within the awakened mind (being, soul). Such a soul is nothing but a vessel of the knowledge that occurs naturally and spontaneously.

Being connected to the vessel of knowledge does not mean to follow the vessel or the form but to be able to perceive it within oneself and to absorb the knowledge from the very vessel, with only one purpose: to contain that knowledge within, live that knowledge, and to gradually integrate it into one's natural being – becoming the selfless vessel of free flow and self-expression. The more we surrender into the selfless flow of being, the deeper we realise the self, and the subtler is the knowledge we perceive from within.

If one's mind is rooted in complication, then such a mind will emanate and manifest complicated forms of knowledge. Such a mind cannot know of or imagine the subtler forms of advanced knowledge. Such minds thus remain oblivious to such forms of teaching/learning until the right time. Original Siddha Teachings are based on the subtle connection with the living vessel of Siddha Knowledge – a teacher, who can be in a physical form or in subtler forms. Such Teaching emphasises 'living teaching', which is a subtle emanation of a living organism who has undergone refinement and transformation. This is why such a being is called a 'vessel'. In such advanced forms of teaching/learning, words matter only to a degree; what matters more is the conscious connection, the state of selfless being, gratitude, and the intention to refine self. True learning is when one perceives the subtle truth through tangible words, when the words are alive and producing an effect on the subtle and physical being of a recipient. Such a phenomenon is called the spiritual transmission of a pure vessel.

Pure Spiritual Transmission is not burdened by intentions, emotions or thoughts. That is why it remains pure and transmits the Ultimate, which is the foundation or the root out of which such words or knowledge emanations stream. An ability to connect the Subtle forms of Knowledge into a sequence of tangible words, abstract verbal patterns and modalities is the quality of an evolved teacher who is not only emanating in silence but is able to selflessly convey the meaning through vibrant words and enlightened logic. Such a being is often considered to be an evolved teacher or a being whose natural quality is effortless teaching and guidance, whether through trivial situations, friendly talks, laughter, or a flow of multiple ways of self-expression, serious talks and discussions. This is the freedom of self-expression and effortless teaching that can only be recognised and realised by mature souls seeking inner breakthroughs, unconditional liberation and spiritual being.

Shaktipat Stream is the stream of living transmission and being that Jivanmukti represents. For those who solely understand the limited forms of spirituality, such Being or emanation cannot be deciphered or recognised for what it is. Subtle forms of Spiritual Learning are for the beings who have refined gross-emotional distortions and conscious afflictions within the self and are able to perceive the self on a subtler level.

The main point of Shaktipat Stream is connection, invocation and the support of the higher frequency of Being, which helps one to refine the self on a subtler level and to unfold subtler forms of knowledge within. Shaktipat Stream has to be recognised for what it is, not through the power of one's logical mind, but through the power of one's meditative absorption and natural recognition of the subtle being within. This recognition is the direct experience of awakening, which, through the constant connection with the vessel of the living knowledge and teaching, leads one to gradual refinement and to deeper levels of self-realisation and spiritual advancement.

The awakening itself is the realisation of the natural being within, yet this alone is not enough to advance, and one needs to go through a long period of disillusionment and refinement. True refinement would then lead one to simplicity, selflessness, and the very realisation of the subtler being in which one would eventually establish oneself. Such Being is beyond time, and thus, is called the immortal one. Such Being is imbued with the natural gratitude to the flow of life within and without, is naturally selfless, humble and empowered by blissful contentment and Knowledge of the Reality and creation. Such Being eventually becomes the very living vessel of that which one contains within the Being and which emanates naturally outwards.

True knowledge is so subtle that it is perceived as blissful emptiness. It is empty yet absolutely wholesome and fulfilling; it is spontaneous and unpredictable yet absolutely balanced and in harmony within itself. Such knowledge embodies time, life, and the space of existence as one emanation of eternal consciousness – unlimited yet fully organised into a perfect multidimensional flow of creation and order within this creation; simple yet multi-layered; omnipresent yet invisible; mighty yet absolutely humble; clear yet flexible; advanced yet simple.

INVOKING

REALITY

SIDDHA SHAKTIPAT: THE GATES OF REALITY

Q: What is shaktipat, who can give it, and what does it mean to receive it?

A: Words do not describe what shaktipat is. It is but grace which is always there; but if one is unrefined and impure, then one is not aware of this constant grace, and thus, one falls into delusion and projections. True knowledge, from shaktipat, is self-protected by purity. If there is no purity, then one cannot perceive the grace. If the vessel is corrupt, then Knowledge cannot be born within it.

In truth, no one can 'give' it. Shaktipat is the Being emanating and invoking the Self (Reality) within the limited embodied consciousness. Shaktipat is always there, as is Existence. Those who understand this, are the embodiment of Shaktipat, of Reality, of Existence.

When one's consciousness is awakened to self-evolution and refinement, one is able to observe what is transitory and what is permanent. By establishing oneself in what is permanent, one becomes That, and That contains all the power in potentiality that is not bound to our usual selfish pursuits. Receiving shaktipat from someone who is able to guide one through the process of refinement is key. Shaktipat activates the process of refinement and leads one to the letting go of the victimised self which clings selfishly. It thus, potentially brings the realisation of the selfless Being.

Q: How did you self-realise? Do you have a Siddha Master? I know that we do not need anyone to self-realise, but in your case, was it all through Siddha teachings or through yourself?

A: Life is a flow of being through various experiences, and the change of the body does not mark the end of this flow, as existence and evolution always continues. It is silly to assume that one achieves spiritual realisation within one fragment of this flow (in one life/incarnation) merely because of perceiving oneself as special or by having a connection to something superficial. One either reaches this level through inner evolutionary maturity, which is selflessness and purity itself, and realises oneself through it, or one only dreams and glides along the surface.

Most people dream and glide along the surface, cultivating hypocrisy and superficiality, dreaming of supernatural powers and the effects of enlightenment. The wise ones mature in silence and through natural simplicity and stillness. They shun the tinsel of superficiality and thus, are pure and mature enough to contain true knowledge. They gradually refine and thus, manifest true knowledge as purity within, as their Natural Being. Absorbed into this Being, they are known as realised and evolved beings. They do not carry the social tags of being self-realised or enlightened or special. They move on in their evolution silently and gracefully towards an existence which is hard to imagine for complex minds, an existence of cumulative intelligence and blissful Being, where the body becomes immortal and then dissolves, and where the world remains a beautiful dream of that time that never existed. When one is That, Reality is one, and all within it is That too.

4

So, what gurus, self-realisations or dreams of enlightenment are we talking about? One simply becomes the vessel of knowledge, the teaching, and the learning, or does not.

Siddha teaching is not limited by the word 'siddha'. The purity and selflessness beyond human moral standards are at its core. It is grasped by simple minds and pure hearts, and remains occulted, mystical or magical for human fools. Time offers each being an opportunity to be pure, yet only those rare ones, in this day and age, appreciate such a gift of Siddha knowledge and Siddha teaching.

The majority are victims of false teachings – because they are the victims of their own ignorance and imagination, fools and slaves of the power which they project outside of the self. Aiming in the darkness, they hope for salvation. That is why Siddha knowledge is known to very few, while the rest fall prey to charlatans who hide behind names; it is all a game of one's own mind, where nothing like that actually exists but in the dream of the limited consciousness.

Q: How do I flow? How do I integrate?

A: Do not 'do'. Live life and learn from it with awareness. Observe the flow you shape within the current of your own limited consciousness and understand the limitations. Eventually, that which binds you becomes the path to your liberation. Thus, never turn away from yourself. Face yourself and understand your own distortions – your weaknesses, strengths, inclinations, and the reasons for them.

The process is more about observing and cultivating stillness and a pure perception in order to observe the inner corruption rather than actually doing anything through spiritual action. On this path, there is only one reward: Pure, Unlimited Awareness, Being, and a deep connection with the creation as the Natural World. When this is present, the man-made illusion falls off and there is a natural flow of Being – life which is unobscured and untouched by the man-made illusion.

Q: *I have been hurt by shakti before. Is it possible to be destroyed by it altogether?*

A: Shakti is the power of Consciousness. It is that through which Consciousness operates in the multiple realities that are manifested by it. One cannot be hurt by it. One can only be hurt by the inner personal corruption that can exist within the dimensions of the individual and collective consciousness.

In this age of darkness, people are hurt through their own victimised perspectives. Victimisation is the cancer of the collective and of our societies. Thus, self-punishment prevails, as does the misinterpretation of reality, and personal ambitions that are rooted in a corrupt and discontented identity that leads to inner suffering. Suffering happens because the individual self is not connected with the Subtle Ultimate Being. To awaken means to reconnect with it, and to the deep experience of realignment with the blissful and conscious intelligent Self-Being, which fulfils one naturally through eternal contentment. It is always there at all times. Become aware of it and gain contentment.

Q: I have just experienced an outburst of emotion after watching your video transmission.

A: This is because all you know of as your current reality are emotions. If your space were free from the imbalanced emotional and thought vibrations, then all you would perceive is the equanimous blissful Being – the Ultimate.

True spirituality is not about transitory or incoherent experiences, whether spiritual or related to the mundane bodily existence. It is about awakening to the Ultimate Being/Existence, beyond the transitory and limited existence of the body, and about gradually and naturally aligning it with the inner refinement and bodily transformation that eventually changes one's entire understanding of being, space, time, life, existence and existential priorities. This is why the way of true spirituality has been presented in this world for human beings as Authentic Yoga or the Siddha Path (please do not confuse it with anything currently known or presented as Yoga or under the name of Siddha, since this is simply a disgrace), or in other words, the integrated way of realigning the self back with the Natural Being and existence, a way that is perceived as a gradual natural awakening and refinement and evolution of spiritual intelligence in the body. To come across and understand such a unique authentic path within, one is to mature by letting go internally of all the subtle connections with the illusionary existence while cultivating selflessness and simplicity and dealing with day-to-day activities.

The more you empower emotions, the less you can perceive contentment and the Reality, and the more your spirituality will be of a limited nature as a result of your own projection and reflection.

Q: Can you explain the difference between awakening and activation?

A: Activation can either be temporary or permanent. In the latter case, the terms can be seen as synonyms. True awakening is when one's consciousness turns within, and one's entire body is able to reconnect with the root, with the Ultimate Being.

This experience brings instant Yoga, the experience of samadhi, and enlightens the subtle. Through the gradual refinement of this connection, one is able to enlighten the physical too, to understand the essence of existence, to free the self from emotional and other karmic baggage, and to continue one's evolution further in a subtler form. One is able to understand what the true exit from this illusion is and thus, one is able to conclude the unconscious existence in the body.

The path is individual and is always within. Awakening happens when one is able to turn one's conscious power within and understand the way that one creates everything within the self, and to connect it to the space of existence. It is far from New Age bullshit.

Q: Can I please receive the blessing of Diksha Shaktipat?

A: You, and the majority of those who watch my videos, have no clue or understanding of what true Being and emanation is. You have preconceived ideas and concepts about spirituality and see everything through a prism of obscured vision.

The Siddha Path will remain unknown to the majority of the current population. These transmissions are not solutions to anything, nor are they energy boosts or energy sharing. Their purpose is to help you understand that you are connected to the Ultimate within yourself, and that you can reconnect, through absorption and stillness, at any time. With time, this may naturally cause you to have more awareness of life so that, through a long and difficult refinement period, you may come to understand the essence of existence.

Hardly anyone can grasp the teaching due to a lack of maturity, due to righteousness, to holding on to preconceived man-made ideas and concepts about spirituality, and due to a deeply wounded perspective of the self. We can only come to realisation when we awaken to the Natural World and come to live in harmony with the self and the world. The world then becomes a beautiful organic learning environment and life experience. The videos aim to offer a glimpse of this Natural Being.

Q: What is the difference between guided meditation and meditation done without guidance?

A: True meditation arises from the Being, when one discovers the natural mind – Being – within the self. True Initiation is for the purpose of letting the other experience true effortless meditation – Yoga, samadhi, equanimity. With time and with refinement, the depth and length of this natural meditation prolongs, and it starts permeating all areas of one's life.

Meditation is not a practice, and it never can be. Either you are meditation, or you are not (yet). All other voluntary and forceful efforts are made due to the lack of awareness about true spirituality and evolution. Those who discover, by chance and by grace, the actual equanimity of one's being, stop looking for any spiritual boost from the outside. Such beings dwell in inner contentment, cultivating inner simplicity, selflessness and silence.

Most of the things that people practice, blow up their egos and make them think they are special. But the refinement element is always missing. One steps onto a true path within, only by the grace of inner maturity and through selflessness, not otherwise.

Guided practices are not complete spiritual transmissions; they are the transmissions of those people's limited consciousness. Such practices, much like watching television or listening to music, have a hypnotic effect on people, where the mind falls into passivity and partial unawareness. Such a state, without awareness, can be quite dangerous, and in some cases can cause entity-possession and hallucination if the channel of such transmission is impure or in contact with any occult practices (as most of the current gurus are).

True kundalini awakening is about the expansion of awareness and awakening to the equanimous Self-Being. From that point on, the actual journey within begins, where one's experience expands and one's body transforms.

Q: Does this transmission also work for psychic protection?

A: This transmission awakens one to the understanding that all the negativity comes from within. Once one realises this, one becomes aware of one's own transitory and limited nature out of which all the illusionary emotional and thought phenomena arise. In this way, one learns about how the inner waves of negativity are related to one's emotions and to the way they arise within one's conscious space, even if it may appear as if it is through someone external to oneself that such things arise.

By taking full responsibility for one's own existence, one stops blaming the projected world and learns to observe oneself, one's own reactions and how one can work with them. In this way, one becomes more cautious and protects oneself by keeping one's lower nature under the supervision of one's consciousness, and one tries to refine the self and to let go of all of one's (and other people's) thoughts, ideas, concepts, beliefs, etc. These distorted tendencies feed off of one's thoughts and emotions and veil one's perception of reality by making one believe that there is a life outside of one's own consciousness. If one does not come out of such beliefs, thoughts and emotions, and if one keeps on feeding them from within, they will start haunting one and creating the impression within oneself that one is weak, disempowered or a victim of this world. The more one gets victimised by one's own thoughts, projections, interpretations and emotions, the more one perceives the occult (hidden) presence within one's space of being, and the more one sabotages one's life.

True protection is found through awareness, and by taking full responsibility for every moment in life, for every emotion and reaction, and by doing the hard work of refining the self. Through inner refinement, one gradually rids oneself of all sorts of negative emotions and pseudo-ideas. Then, one dwells in contentment and the blissful Being, which becomes one's spiritual presence – emanation, free from thoughts and emotions. This is the true protection.

Q: Can I awaken and evolve through worshipping Shiva?

You can worship Shiva if you understand the essence of Shiva rather than the form. However, how can one understand the essence of what one does not know within themselves? You can only project your higher self onto a holy form of Shiva for a while, until you deepen your state of self. Life is neutral and has no meaning. We arrive at experience, and if we do it consciously, then we grow in our understanding of the self and of all that which is around the self. The point is not to move anywhere in life, but to learn to feel each moment of life's experience in depth.

Q: Does dispassion ultimately lead to spiritual freedom?

A: Having a dispassionate attitude is not enough, as your awareness has to be awakened first in order to perceive, as a neutral observer, certain emotional responses within so that you can then transform those responses and understand the deeper root causes and distortions within your limited consciousness. It is hard work, and most of this work comprises one's 'spiritual sadhana' – the refinement and transformation process. Transformation happens within awakening, and the awakening to subtler and subtler Self-Being happens within transformation. Mastery over the self is nothing but the complete transformation of, and freedom from, those gross distortions. Such a freedom vibrates spiritual bliss and power.

Q: As I meditated, I concentrated on my brow and a white light appeared so that I could not open my eyes. I felt like I was floating in the air and my body was bent like a bow. I started uncontrollably repeating an 'ummm' sound and cried. What does this all mean?

A: These are all various transitory phenomena coming from the illusory self. When one is exposed to highly-spiritual vibrations of the unconditional selfless Being, all that is false, delusional and hidden, comes to the surface. As long as all this comes up, there is no true meditation. True meditation is absolute absorption, silence, stillness and void. As long as there is any comparison, envy, or any man-made human reality with all its ideas, then there is no meditation, nor awareness of the Natural Being.

The first step in spiritual evolution is to refine the self so that it unfolds the true essence of Being. As long as projection, memory, imagination and ideas of the self and others permeate one's existence, that existence will be a false one, created by a corrupt mind. The moment the mind discovers its natural, unconditional Being, one awakens to Yoga and meditation effortlessly. This is why Yoga and meditation cannot be practiced. Practices are for the man-made spirituality and its practitioners, but for Reality, such things are absurd.

Q: There are lots of misleading things happening with spirituality these days, especially with kundalini. Only siddha gnosis can save humanity from the darkness. Siddhas struggled a lot before attaining enlightenment. Those who drifted away from the Siddha tradition forgot that everything they were seeking was actually within themselves.

A: This is spot on and very true. Most of the people in the spiritual marketplace are occultists and spiritual predators. If one realises this, then one will come across genuine knowledge that starts to unfold from within. Most people who taste some movement in their subtle bodies or some occult presence assume that they are awakened or enlightened and may even proclaim themselves to be gurus. This is indeed falsehood. Siddha Science is pure in its essence and self-protected against corruption. Only Pure vessels may contain such pure Being and teaching. True spiritual science is very simple yet is hard to grasp for distorted and corrupt minds.

Q: Many times, I fall asleep after receiving your transmission. Why does this happen?

A: This happens because your mind cannot withstand (with your waking-consciousness) the deep sleep waves. In other words, one is not yet able to perceive the Ananda Kosha whilst being awake. When most people sleep, they experience dreams or go into a deep unconscious state. Yogis can perceive all of these states (which are normal for a human being as well as for those who are beyond such states) as one existence, through their awakened awareness. Over time, and by awakening to your essence more, you will be able to experience the blissful equanimous being whilst being fully alert.

Q: Do you ever initiate people or have mantras that relate to the Divine Mother and that help to connect to Siddha Being?

A: A mantra has to be activated by a true Siddha guru, and there are no such gurus in the marketplace of today that you browse through. Live from your own level of consciousness and go through what you are to go through. In this day and age, the majority of the world is possessed or ruled by lower-realm entities; and all those who portray themselves to be gurus and spiritual beings are just magicians, low tantriks, and demonic entities in a human form.

If you wonder why this is the case, it is because this is the age where these beings are in control and are driven by power, money and self-gratification. It is the time of corruption and of witnessing this corruption through various forms. Spirituality is no exception. On the contrary, it is a means for such beings to enslave and control others through an established, false spiritual hierarchy. All is deception. True spirituality is so far from anything that you hear or know about, and the majority will never come across it in their lifetime because there is no demand for it nor the slightest connection to it.

Why people get attracted to falsehood is because they themselves are driven by the same principle. When one is ready and pure within, one is able to recognise the true Siddha teaching – one is naturally drawn to it. Until that happens, people will explore through various low spiritual sciences and take them for spiritual truth or for the path of evolution. This happens because their motive is not to self-refine but to gain power, as they are coming from the victimised self-perception of reality. When such a perception is present, true Siddha Knowledge and presence cannot be recognised nor fully known, nor can true grace – Shaktipat – be perceived.

Q: Who were these ageless yogis you speak of? None of the Tibetan yogis in the Dzogchen/Mahamudra tradition who achieved Rainbow bodies lived exceptionally long or stopped aging. Your definition of Shaktipat also does not make sense. Shaktipat is the descent of Divine Power, meaning, Shakti or the Holy Spirit.

A: Time presents us with a chance to experience and to learn. Respect time and understand the essence of your life experience before you go into judgement or wonder about the experiences of others. Refine yourself from negative emotions and reactions through the cultivation of stillness, selflessness and purity, and then you may begin to approach the level of maturity to be able to make that immortality your reality. So far, it is not your reality, and there is no need for you to buy into anything. Just learn to trust life and live it wholesomely, selflessly, and without entanglement and drama. Then, knowledge will naturally unfold within.

Q: Can you please explain what selflessness is and how it joins with equanimity, contentment and humility?

A: You must understand that everything is wholesome, even if it does not appear to you as such at any given point in time. Understand that the only thing you can pursue is your own purity and selflessness. When one understands this, all the illusions fall away, and one will mature and become ready for the true knowledge of Reality. Such knowledge is beyond words and is always present as the subtle, pure, unconditional and selfless existence.

Q: What are the reasons for an awakening that does not lead to refinement?

A: True awakening always leads to refinement. Even if one is not awakened, one very slowly refines through life circumstances. Awakening leads one to a more intense conscious refinement through the appearance of more intense challenges in life. These challenges are the dormant distortions within one's consciousness. The consciousness that is awakened tries to bring all of this up to the surface by manifesting people and circumstances that trigger various emotional reactions within one's body and being. In this way, one is able to see what is 'Being' and what the transitory emanation of self is.

No amount of words can describe the moment of actual experience. True awakening gives the experience of Yoga through one being in equanimity to the degree one is able to perceive it. But during awakening, one is not established in this equanimity, and so one has to use the experience of absorption into the self for self-refinement and inner transformation. This is the path.

Q: I want to learn Siddha techniques. Can you help me do this?

A: There are no Siddha techniques. There is only the Siddha space-like, blissful, equanimous Being, which is knowledge, bliss and power. Yoga is not about tricks or techniques. It is about the Ultimate Reality and Being of Self. Once this is understood, no tricks, rituals or shows are needed.

Q: Should I practice yoga exercises?

A: You may exercise if you feel like it, or walk, or have warm tea with ginger if you feel cold. Yet, this has nothing to do with Yoga. Yoga is a Being. All other activities or actions and non-actions should arise from that Being, and only then is one a yogi.

Otherwise, exercises are simply exercises and can be used to keep one warm and less stagnant. You may always clean your house, walk and dance; these are other forms of exercise that help your body stay less stressed and more relaxed. The point or goal of every exercise is to feel that contentment or bliss of relaxation once you have finished doing it. Exercise is, in other words, the exhaustion of stagnant energy.

Energy flows out and is exhausted naturally through proper breathing, relaxation, being outdoors and through intellectual activities; and it has very little to do with the amount of calories you consume or the hours you exercise. The best way to balance our energy flow is by being deeply relaxed into the Being, absorbed and blissful, and by breathing deeply and being content. Stagnation on the energetic level comes from overthinking, imbalanced emotional responses (for instance, overly empathising or fearing the loss of someone or something) and overeating or eating that which blocks and stagnates the body. Moderation is a discipline that arises from wisdom, and wisdom arises from equanimity – which is Yoga.

Q: How can I practice self-control?

A: Self-control cannot be learnt. It is a state of mind. It comes spontaneously when consciousness (kundalini) is awakened and has purified one's mental and physical aspects to some degree. When this happens, it results in inner contentment, where one is absorbed within, and when one knows that, even though the external world can be enjoyed, it cannot be compared to the pleasure of the thoughtless-mind that is absorbed in the Self.

Q: How can I cultivate absorption? Should I focus more on absorption or on understanding and healing the emotional issues within?

Once there is nothing on your mind, absorption is but natural. Learn to see your own restlessness and projections and try to contain inner power through stillness. This means not going outwards in thought or emotions. Then, you will understand naturally.

Q: Can you explain what happens during a shaktipat transmission?

A: Transmission means that one is pulled into the space of the enlightened consciousness through a mutual connection of awareness. The meeting of the guru and the student is just an illusion, since in the space of the Self there is no separation, it is just a vibration of being that is awakened to the Self. That is why the final understanding is that there is no guru and no student, but only the ever-flowing and empty Being.

Transmission can also be verbal, although the actual transmission is what is behind the words. Real shaktipat transmission is the constant pouring of grace or flow of Ultimate Being to the manifested self. If the channels are clear and aware, then one perceives it, but if the channel is polluted and full of concepts, emotions and ideas, then the Transmission is still there but its fruits will only be seen later on, once the load of concepts and ideas, emotions and thoughts are consciously or forcefully let go of.

When the vessel is clear, the grace is perceived. That is why the body – karma – is to be refined through awakening. Awakening means the opening of grace through inner maturity and through the process of letting go of the gross impediments in consciousness. Enlightenment refers to when one's being becomes the constant shaktipat through the inner purity and unobstructed flow of Being in the body. Such a presence enlightens and uplifts effortlessly.

Q: You sound as if you are an elitist by saying that awakening can only happen through the grace of shaktipat. And for those going through difficulty during their awakening, it does not make any sense to say to them that their awakening is not authentic or valid. I also believe that many people are having spontaneous awakenings because of the evolutionary times we live in. So why do you claim that only a master can awaken a practitioner?

A: Opinions may vary, but the essence is neutral and is as it is. When you see deeper, you will understand that what I say does not come from the point of view of trying to separate reality but rather, from the point of neutral observation. If something is red, then it is red; if something is black then it is black. Does it matter if one considers red to be superior to black?

True awakening is a conscious shift that results in bio-spiritual transformation. It is not the science of either 'your awakening' or 'my awakening', but the science that is just there. You are either that science in your own being or you are an idea, a thought about the science. It is the same with Yoga – you are either Yoga or not Yoga, either samadhi or not.

When there is Knowledge, words fail, as true Knowledge is self-protected and only unfolds in pure vessels. The purity of the individual defines what depth of knowledge, spiritual power and radiation unfolds from within. Words always mislead, and they are understood through each individual mind through its own distorted perception. If one is able to go beyond the words, it happens only because one's being is refined and pure, so that that purity connects to the Ultimate Flow.

Experiences can be forced by inducing them to happen, but purity and self-born knowledge cannot be bought or forced into existence. Kundalini awakening is not about invoking an experience; it is about reconnecting with the Ultimate Being. If the process is misunderstood, then it leads to delusion.

People have a difficult time during awakening only because of the ancestral, occult, and karmic afflictions that affect them when there is no authentic Param-Para. Spontaneous awakening without grace, brings up all the karmic experiences and pain, and only through proper guidance can one come out of this process enlightened. The majority of people perish or get tangled more with the reality while attempting to go through this process. This happens due to their lack of awareness about the actual path and the science of spiritual evolution. But there is no fault in this, as everything is correct in its time and place. Every experience we have is of the nature of teaching and learning. The more we cultivate purity and selflessness and understand that there is still so much to learn, the more self-knowledge unfolds within us, as we get a chance for further guidance beyond our expectations of name and form. The more preconceived our ideas are about what awakening and enlightenment are, and about how the guidance should appear in our lives, the more corrupt the form of this guidance we shall receive. To each his own way...

Q: Is it possible to follow you and receive your shaktipat while also following another path?

A: There is only one evolution and one path, so there is no requirement for it to be named or labelled in any way. External paths may appear as many, but only until the spark within oneself is active and one thus perceives oneself beyond the multiple identities and paths of the past. The separate aspects of the self (the intellect, and so on) have a path, but Self is Being – so what path does it have?

Q: What is celibacy?

A: True celibacy is one's ability to stay in stillness while deeply absorbed, where the mind-consciousness is still, unmovable and does not wander, project or analyse. Then, one perceives one's Natural Being, virgin-like purity and Beingness. When the conscious power does not project outwardly, it does not cling to the external or to the projected, and thus, no energy is drained.

When the emotions and thoughts are scattered, and when consciousness holds information within itself actively, it means that one is not experiencing spiritual celibacy. Only when one is absorbed and still is one truly celibate.

Q: Where should I focus my eyes in order to get the maximum reception from your transmission?

A: The fact that you are aware of the transmission connects you with the field. Concentrate within, relax into your spine, and make sure that your facial muscles are relaxed too. No matter whether you think it is or not, your consciousness is still being affected, so you may experience an instant or gradual shift (depending on your openness). You will be learning to accommodate this shift within your body and being and live this shift through the expanded awareness of your everyday life while your perception of the self and life gradually changes.

Q: I have researched, done lots of sadhana and gained perfect and real experience on, and written a book about, kundalini shakti. You will get all your answers to all your questions about kundalini shakti by reading this book.

A: Socrates said that 'I know that I know nothing', and he said this from the standpoint of having true experience. This is also the understanding of all wise human beings in this world. They simply share their presence and wisdom without taking any pride in the act of doing so. Selflessness and simplicity are the qualities of those who truly know.

My book, *Siddha Param-Para* may not answer all your logic-based questions (although it may do this too), but it can pull you into the essence of your being. One cannot know Yoga, Shiva-Shakti, or Being, since one either is Yoga, Shiva-Shakti and Being or is only on the journey attempting to know that state. After that, comes the emptiness of silent Being, which is completeness. Wise people do not take pride in their mental and intellectual achievements but dwell in the contentment of Self-Being. This Being exists within us but is concealed from the proud ones, because the truth is open only to those who live through the simple and most powerful, conscious, blissful Being, which is empty for the world yet contains the world within the self. In that Being, the realisation of 'I know that I know nothing' arises.

Q: I started having pain in my crown chakra after listening to you.

A: This path is not for entertainment, and it is not another drug. When you feel something, it means that you get a glimpse of what is beyond the body. You have touched your root – the blissful equanimous Reality of the Self. Now, you have to refine it. This task requires a deeper understanding, inner dedication, and the courage to let go of all the rubbish that you have thought of as the self and spirituality thus far. It is easier said than done, as spirituality is about integration and not about one-sided theoretical learning. It starts with the experience and requires a lot of internal work. If one understands the process, then one understands the simplicity of it all and trusts the flow within. One learns the essence of life and eventually liberates the self by exiting this reality consciously. This is the path of Siddhas.

Q: Some enlightened Gurus are giving Shaktipat to their disciples. What is your take on this?

A: By whose standards are these masters enlightened? The enlightened know the enlightened, beggars only know beggars, and kings mingle with other kings; a thief knows a thief; a corrupt mind knows another corrupt mind, and an ambitious mind recognises another ambitious mind and connects with it; a restless mind cannot recognise the still mind unless it becomes still itself.

People do all sorts of things. That which is the Natural Being and emanation cannot be faked or performed. If one wants to be a king in the human world, then one cannot be a king in the world of higher Being.

In the world based on action, the Being is occulted. In the world of higher Being, that Being causes vibration, which is action through inaction. This is why truly evolved beings are hidden, and why those who consider themselves to be evolved (but in reality are not), act like kings on Earth. True kings, however, are like truly evolved beings; they operate in disguise through the power of their Being and not by acting openly. The present age is not the right time to know of such dignity. Rather, it is the age of facing degradation and corruption. One either is Knowledge or is merely acting like Knowledge. The power of the act extinguishes and exhausts, but the power of Being is inexhaustible.

Q: I am determined to open my third eye, so I have been watching your video transmissions for three days. But now I have a heavy head, cannot sleep, and have heart palpitations and anxiety. What has happened?

A: Do not overdo the transmissions. They are not another drug! They are there to support the people in their refinement and spiritual evolution who are prepared and are genuine adepts. They require observation and contemplation of the self while working with one's inner programs of victimisation, emotional triggers, reactions and distortions. They are not for entertainment but are a gateway to one's inner world and to a deeper understanding of oneself. You should drink more water and try to live a more balanced lifestyle that includes plenty of fresh air, walking, and going to bed early and waking up early. Do not sleep during the day but lie down and rest if you are feeling overwhelmed. Stop imagining and dreaming about life, and have clarity and vision while doing what you like in a selfless way. Be grateful for what you have and learn through life in a conscious way with awakened awareness.

Q: If one is able to manifest one's life externally does it mean that one's third eye is open?

A: One first needs to prepare the soil. The prerequisite for spiritual advancement is to have inner purity and to have the desire to refine. Having this, one manifests the opportunity for oneself to come across the truth. It is the degree of purity that defines whether one will recognise this truth or not, as well as how much one can sustain such knowledge within. Understanding things other than in this way is merely speculation and spiritual hallucination.

Q: I disagree with a lot of what you say. I also think that it is important for you to have discernment and not be gullible.

A: Spirituality is beyond agreement and disagreement. It is about the level of awareness that one has. The more we deny, the more we shall face that which we deny. The more we aim at something, the more life shows us how limited, fleeting and insubstantial all of our actions are. Wisdom is born out of awareness. Awareness does not claim that it knows or does not know. It is knowledge and emanation; it is the existence through which various other phenomena appear. To awaken means to become aware of the various subtle phenomena. The way one handles it all defines one's level of evolution. Agreeing or disagreeing with existence does not help. Everyone is in it and everyone perceives it to the degree of their individual awareness at any given time. Thus, time is the best teacher, which guides each and every one of us through this existence and offers the experience that will deepen our individual awareness.

If one is not aware of something so far, it does not mean that it does not exist. Most people choose to live in an illusionary world and that is their choice. It is a temporary thing though, because these illusory bubbles usually burst quickly and reveal the essence of the current day and age and its prevailing dark phenomena. But everyone is able to put on rose-coloured glasses, imagine, create a new bubble, take a pill and fly away.

Q: Why is there a flash of light when I intentionally close my eyes and focus on the centre of my eyebrows. Is it normal for this to occur?

A: You are having a glimpse of the mind's essence. The focus, however, has to be on self-observation and self-refinement. Spiritual phenomena and experiences, even though fascinating at times, are transitory. Look for that experience which lasts – the equanimous, blissful, content yet empty Being. By the grace of your own maturity, simplicity, and selflessness you may come across a true master. Then, your entire perception will change, and true spirituality will unfold gradually. Bookish knowledge and a search that is limited by concepts, someone else's theories, talks and outdated ideas, leads one to spiritual traps, hallucinations, and diversions. Still, everything is correct and happens at the right time.

Q: I apologise for my previous comments. They came at a time when I still did not understand that we create our reality and that we can perceive the flow of life and be responsible for it. I have been reclusive for two years since I first saw your video transmissions and experienced silence and stillness for the first time, but I also want a new life of expansion, truth and real spirituality.

A: You do not need to apologise for anything, for it is through the confrontation with reality that we learn about the self and the reality. One can only see beyond one's veils when one is able to accept the fact that there exist multiple perspectives. The majority of people in this life cannot, and will not, break through their man-made reality, but will fight for and defend their man-made spirituality and ambitious spiritual practices until they one day awaken. But even their false and delusional (and often occult-driven) awakening is not the true spiritual awakening from ignorance, but on the contrary, is the awakening to the illusionary multidimensional reality within which they have no intelligence or spiritual capacity to navigate through it, and are thus driven by various subtle entities, whether demonic or angelic, whether gods or deities, into more illusion and subtle bondage. It is difficult to ever break through such phenomena in which the whole world is engrossed, unless, by grace and at the right evolutionary moment, one is able to awaken to all this and start the tedious process of self-refinement.

Do not look for truth in the manifested world, since the truth is existence – which is empty, blissful, pure as the void itself, and absolutely powerful in its humility. All these false notions of light and of darkness are of the man-made reality, and as such, they are of an illusionary nature. The true void is that which all light and darkness are born from, and so only that space is the canvas of various realities and dimensions. For the human mind, it is empty, but it is the most wholesome existence, one which no human can contain within or even imagine because they are engrossed in their little world of happiness and suffering. Let it go and dwell in simplicity, for there is no truth in this world or in any other subtler reality. The simple awareness of this fact, along with the true existence that is within the self, pulls one through various phenomena of the manifested conscious light-matter and defines one's evolutionary status as being either ignorant, or being the one who is deeply aware and connected in awareness through all illusions so that they remain wholesome and eternal.

Learn to let go and withdraw the mind into natural silence, beyond the projections and shadows of this realm. If you strive, then soon you will have silence... later contentment, and later still, blissful Being.

Q: What do you think about the teachings of Mooji?

A: I do not think about anyone's teachings. Question everything and check its validity only through the experience of your own being. True teaching – inner knowledge – arises through inner absorption and the evolution of one's being through self-refinement, selflessness, and the deeper understanding of the root causes of one's illusions, and it has to culminate in one's establishment in the true, blissful, unconditional Being. Such Being is to be integrated into one's life and one's actions, so that such actions leave no emotional or mental impressions and are therefore free in their nature. If any teaching is about this, then it is a genuine teaching. Beautiful and wise talks by others do not take one far.

The sign of having correct experience, correct knowledge, and being on the correct path within, is when there is experience and an internal shift, a transformation and the discovery of the inner power based on Self-Being and absorption (samadhi), and the ability to refine the self through this absorption while staying in a humble and selfless yet confident and autonomous state. May those who are genuine and mature, discover such a path through simplicity and honesty, come across such a teaching and awaken to the Being of the self.

Q: What is the ego? Do we need to destroy it?

A: The ego, in the negative sense, is that which obstructs the free creative flow of the self (the expression of the self in all forms). Within the individual consciousness is an illusion in the form of an obscure perception and limited comprehension of experience. There is nothing wrong with the manifestation (nor with any experience within the manifestation) if the experience leaves no trace on the individual consciousness and does not create a recollection, longing or projection.

The ego – the self-identity – is the very seed of our existence and reason for it. What matters is the level of self-realisation and awareness that we have, through this identity. In order to be free, we have to experience the natural mind, which is free from projections and recollections. The ego is our past that consciousness tries to bring up. It wants to bring it up for only one purpose – to be free from it (to see it more clearly and to neutralise its impressions). By realising that our experience is the product of the ego (or the distortions within consciousness), and by experiencing the natural mind in its stillness and neutrality, we can understand that there is nothing wrong with the experience or the manifestation but with the consciousness and its tendencies, inclinations and assumptions (judgments) towards one experience over others.

The ego is that which recollects, analyses, judges, projects, and is of an anxious and ambitious nature. True Being, natural mind, or whatever you wish to call it, is neutral, still, empty, equanimous and blissful. It is creativity in potentiality. Once you experience the natural mind-being, you automatically know that which is of a transitory nature.

All the emotions and thought-waves are distortions of the mind-being, yet they come from the Being and are inseparable from the Being. You cannot destroy them or run away from them, just as you cannot run away from the self. You can only understand the nature of consciousness, which manifests the illusion from the essence/space of the self. You can only learn to understand that space itself vibrates and produces the phenomena, and you can only master the self as the space that vibrates and manifests – you can subside the waves within the self and be. This is the path of Siddha Kundalini Yoga or Natural Spiritual Being.

Q: How did you become enlightened?

A: Forget enlightenment. Cultivate purity and selflessness; cultivate Self-Being and cut through illusions. Then, you shall evolve. Evolution is eternal, but at the moment, evolution is about self-refinement, so do not look into other people's gardens but cultivate your own. Do not waste time on speculation and wondering but discipline yourself and observe yourself. Discard negative and weak points within, and you will then see beyond the rigid and the obscured.

Q: On my spiritual path I met a genuine shaman/avadhuta/master who had powers and worked with everything which you speak of as 'superficial', but it was for the benefit of others and not for displaying his powers. There are also several famous Mahasiddhas who displayed powers and shared rituals and spells for everyday purposes, such as Dattatreya. Also, many Mahasiddhas worked with yoginis and with other spirits.

A: True Siddha Being is hardly known at all to the world. People who use the word 'Siddha' or other such terms might not represent the essence of Siddha or the authenticity of such Being. True Siddha Beings may live within but beyond the creation; they do not interfere with the world that deludes itself and punishes the self. True Siddhas do not interfere with the world, nor do they help anyone. They emanate that Being that is hard to imagine, a Being that can only be perceived. Through their presence (even when it is not known directly and physically), mature beings evolve and refine.

Siddhas, master the creation and definitely have a mechanism to control it, but they do not interfere with it. They are not magicians nor healers who interact with the masses nor want to help them. They allow creation to go its way according to the natural cycles. As long as delusion persists, true knowledge about Siddhas will remain veiled. Your ideas are based on what people think or imagine and what the public writes about Siddhas. None of these people have ever come across a true Siddha, nor will they in this day and age.

Q: You are a sane voice in a circus full of so-called teachings.

A: Whether it is a circus, hell or heaven, or anything else, if you understand that this realm is a realm in which there is nothing much to pursue, then you should pursue the Natural Being and the True Reality and cultivate it within the self through stillness and absorption. Abstain from judgement, because it is a fact that everything is what it is, and nothing needs to be done about it. It is all a result of the collective, and with time, it will refine and change. But it is all beyond the control of the individual's mind, so focus on the self, have discipline, and self-refine. Do not disperse your mind by wondering why things are the way they are or by trying to do something about it.

KUNDALINI AWAKENING & BIO-SPIRITUAL TRANSFORMATION

Q: Is kundalini just a word to describe the process of the activation of the third eye?

A: Kundalini awakening is the awakening of one's consciousness. The physical vehicle becomes the mirror, and later, the fruit of this process. One's limited consciousness is first to be reconnected to the Ultimate Being. Through this, one realises that one's existence is beyond the limitations of one's individual consciousness. Such a realisation results in the activation of the spiritual light-essence that perceives the Ultimate Being in stillness and absorption and cultivates the conscious power within the body. Eventually, such a process leads to the refinement of the limited mind and body. This is Siddha alchemy.

New Age concepts of the third eye, its activation, and of chakras, are incomplete and very misunderstood. This is due to the lack of actual experience and direct knowledge on the subject, which has led to so much speculation as to what it is all about.

Our physical body has a chamber, which is in the brain. Though it is not all about the physical glands, the upper glands in the brain undergo activation and transformation, but only due to their being reconnected with the root – the Ultimate Being – within one's limited consciousness. Such reconnection is found in effortless stillness, contentment, and blissful absorption. These are not achievements. They are only the foundation for one's further

35

refinement and transformation, through awareness and observation, and through the cultivation of stillness and absorption. Such effortless, mature, and natural spiritual work throughout one's life leads to bodily transformation and enlightenment.

Hardly anyone experiences such phenomena or has achieved such spiritual accomplishment in this day and age. Instead, people dream of things. And by doing so, they stay in the realm of dreams. When awareness penetrates beyond dreams, and when the dreams are dissolved in the emptiness of the self, one perceives the actual Being. This Being is empty (for the illusion) yet blissful and content in itself. This Being is the root we are to reconnect with through the awakening of consciousness. Through this root, we are to refine that which is limited so that we can experience immortality in the body as we transcend into the immortal Being. This is the science and experience of Siddha Kundalini Yoga and Siddha Tantra.

Q: I have read many books from different spiritual traditions but have not found the answers to my questions, only chaos. I have recently understood that kundalini awakening is a process and not a one-time event, as some claim.

A: In this day and age, there is not a single written testimony that refers to what the process of kundalini awakening actually is, and there are hardly any existing lineages through which the living emanation and transmission are still apparent. The knowledge and sciences of Siddhas are not known; so it is that people only speculate upon them. Original Siddha Tantra is barely known either, and people who claim to be true Siddhas are often low-level tantriks and magicians, with very obscured knowledge. This is why the process and science of kundalini awakening cannot be experienced, and why it is hardly known. Such science also remains obscured by the fact that there are no pure vessels who can contain such knowledge and make it unfold within. The evolutionary level of the current day and age is very low. Thus, there is so much speculation on the topic. People experience spiritual possession, communicate with entities, perform rituals where they think they are communicating with gods, and take psychedelic drugs and herbs that they think are connecting them with the creation, but all these acts are anything but spiritual. What most of these people are experiencing is partial awareness of the subtle body and some movements within it, but such movements can be triggered by occult afflictions (black magic), possessions, occult forces and manipulation. In such paths, there is no purity, and they only lead to further corruption and entanglement. Such sciences are not fully understood and are corrupt; they entangle those who abuse them and apply them ignorantly.

The majority of what you see in the spiritual marketplace is entity possession, evidence of occult manipulation, possession through the use of drugs, psychedelics and other stimulants, and the overstimulation of the subtle body through exercises, stimulants, emotional drama, and through occult or other forms of spiritual possession. It can also happen through someone's conscious intent to affect the body of another person (energy healing), because these people ignorantly submit their will to an impure source devoid of pure transmission and uncorrupted knowledge. All of this happens because of ignorance. People have no eyes to see who is who and what is what, and so they fall prey to the occult, which offers them quick solutions or promises of enlightenment. To experience this is okay, since it is just a stage of one's evolution, but it is not kundalini awakening!

True and complete kundalini awakening is very rare. Some mature beings may awaken and experience something, but if they do not continue to refine the self through life-circumstances, and if they go into escapism, into creative outpourings and self-promulgation, then they stay on the same level, with a very limited understanding of what this science truly is. Our evolution is the evolution of intelligence in the body. It is a very deep and multi-dimensional process. The cultivation of selflessness, purity and simplicity will result in the maturity that one needs in order to comprehend this science. True transmission and shaktipat is there at all times, but if the vessel receiving it is not pure, then one can only perceive it in glimpses and try to interpret it through their limited and unrefined mind. This is why there are so many theories, concepts and spiritual movements. The more ignorance there is, the more variety we get. Everyone goes through their own evolutionary cycle, so the fact that this science is hardly known is as it should be. It is not the right time for this to be common knowledge.

Q: What is the role of the spontaneous kriyas in the process of kundalini awakening?

A: Kriyas are a sign of your subtle being or individual consciousness (which is the reason for the existence of your physical body) reacting to a certain piece of information. Kriyas also happen when someone's evolved consciousness, which has the ability to positively impact another individual consciousness through a mutual connection, comes in contact with you. Some people have the ability to affect one's energy body. Yet, this is not a conclusive sign of a spiritually evolved being. Spiritually evolved beings are selfless, simple, as pure as children, yet wise and clear within. They are emotionally balanced most of the time. Such beings are quite rare at this point in time. They do not allow the world to taint them.

Our subtle body can be partially activated – or, to put it another way, we are aware of it to some degree, but there will still not be complete realignment due to the scatteredness of consciousness on all levels. The goal is to collect consciousness through absorption and start respecting and nurturing one's own Being by bringing conscious power within. This is the refinement process that should result in rejuvenation, subtle and physical healing, and longevity. Longevity is important for further evolution in the body.

Q: Is your transmission helpful only for those who have already awoken their kundalini?

A: Awakening is only the beginning of the process because one has to grow through this awakening into transformation. There is a lot to learn and observe from within, and proper guidance is required for this process. To have an awakened kundalini without a proper understanding of the process of transformation, of space and of the spiritual essence, may mislead and delude one.

Q: Can I accelerate the process of kundalini awakening?

A: Why rush? Is someone chasing us and punishing us if we do not get enlightened on time? The false gurus who spread the idea of rushing for enlightenment, died like everyone else. How come their idea of racing towards enlightenment did not bring them to the status of being an Immortal? Always question everything. Live life consciously and accept it as the closest thing to having a guru. All the rest will come automatically and with more maturity. Do not try to make a star out of a light bulb. Such an experiment will fail. Try to let go of unnecessary worry and of the idea of reserving a special place in heaven for yourself. The less you rush, the more you understand, and the deeper you go within. Take this phrase as a guide: Grace is always there. However, the mind takes time to mature.

Q: What is bio-spiritual immortality? Is the biochemical body made immortal by Param-Para?

A: The body can be enlightened by the process of awakening to the Natural Being, the essence of self, which is the immortal, subtle, conscious being/existence. Refining the subtle being will lead to the eventual refinement and transformation of the physical body. Once refined, the subtle essence becomes immortal, and one's evolution as the subtle being continues. Then, the physical body can be preserved for longer, its longevity being supported by the refined light-essence or 'subtle being'. This is a rare phenomenon in this day and age. The majority of people are deeply imbalanced and ignorant, resulting in the overall sickness and social madness of the day. In this day and age, the majority of people look for the pseudo-spirituality of healing and empowerments, and seek other solutions to fix their miserable lives simply because such spirituality resonates more with their current state of consciousness and bodily existence. True spirituality is hardly known and is for the very, very few.

The book I wrote is just a testimony of Siddha teaching and being that awakens one to such a possibility and expands one's awareness beyond the currently-limited ideas of reality, spirituality, spiritual journey, kundalini awakening, meditation, etc. True awakening is extremely rare, and true refinement and actual perfection, even more so. People play with words nowadays and see spirituality as a business opportunity. This is why they are not ever going to come across it or taste it, as long as they go on fooling themselves and others. Such spirituality is dead. True spirituality is alive and vibrant, and it emanates that which it conveys verbally. True spirituality does not transmit emotions or thoughts, but the very refined Being/Existence. Thus, it effortlessly touches others and transforms them whether they accept it or turn away in ignorance.

Q: I have been working with my Kundalini for the last 8 years and have had both scary and amazing experiences. For the last two years, meditation has become a state of nothingness, and the only thing holding me back are the physical sensations and wandering of the mind. I have body rotation, body vibrations, see geometric shapes with closed or open eyes. Can you explain all this? I'm not complaining. It is like living in a daily meditative state, and life does not affect me the same way anymore.

A: Most people think/believe that if they read books or listen to someone, then they learn and know. This is false. With time, they understand that they have no idea. The spirituality of this day and age is absolute madness, ignorance, hallucination, and self-delusion. If one has no grace, nor the courage to understand this and come out of it, then one encompasses the phenomenon of social madness.

The more one truly knows, the more content one is and has autonomy from the collective madness, which is propelled from the inside of each individual being who emotionally supports and believes in it. Chakras and their symptoms? It is all nonsense. If one has no coherent perception of the self, then one only divides reality even more. One is to mature in order to understand the simplicity of one's being, not the complexity. As long as you are trying to find spiritual knowledge and true answers through your limited human experience that is tied to social, cultural, religious, and pseudo-spiritual ideas and limitations, all you are going to come across is the reflection of these ideas and your own limitations.

How can you come across or recognise true spiritual wisdom if all you know is spiritual delusion and imagination? You are going to either support or disagree with those views, but such an understanding is not based on your direct experience of the actual reality but a delusional understanding of reality through your bodily existence.

What you are experiencing are mere glimpses of the subtle Being/Reality. Such experiences are not coherent, nor are they linked to internal conscious refinement and the evolution of spiritual intelligence. They are thus, like dreams, coming and going. Learn to appreciate being in stillness; cultivate contentment, and with time and maturity, you might start seeing the weeds from the wheat.

Q: Eleven months ago, I activated my kundalini and have gone through many symptoms that, fortunately, have subsided, but I still have a subtle vibration in my body and a ringing in the ears. Can you explain?

A: How do you know you have been activated? Coming to perceive your subtle body through overstimulation does not mean that you have fully awakened. Why follow misleading information on kundalini awakening? Why try to cultivate truth within the context of other people's misconceptions?

True awakening is gradual and smooth, provided one has cultivated simplicity and purity. If not, then one will simply be facing all the rubbish within. How to deal with this? Drop the romantic feelings about spirituality and embrace life. All that which is your life, is your being that is polluted with issues. So, now is the time to start seeing it and refining it. Roll up your sleeves and drop all the ideas of being special. Nothing and no one is special. Special is a word for spiritual dreamers and people obsessed with power, ambition, and spiritual narcissism. Such beings never go beyond the creation, and thus do not understand existence. Your own life will show to you and give you clues about your impurities, the roots of which are to be understood. By doing this, you will be able to see, through your being, how creation comes into play. It is going to take time.

Q: I have been practicing pranayama and bandhas and can feel vibration in my body, but I think there is some blockage in the chakras. Can you please initiate me?

A: The true path is spontaneous – Sahaj. It manifests within and without by the grace of one's own conscious spiritual maturity and simplicity. The path of awakening is not about practicing. It is about the experience of the teaching – Yoga, equanimity, Ultimate Being – within the self, and understanding all that is not the Self (all that is transitory). The body is the fruit and reflection of one's consciousness.

Q: Does the kundalini energy need 'guidance' or does one just need to observe it?

A: Kundalini is more than energy. It is the conscious power of the self. It contains everything we are aware of and are not aware of. Once we go beyond collective thoughts, we perceive the selfless space of the self and everything within that Space. The thing that requires guidance is one's navigation through and out of the self-created illusion of the self. For this, one needs to consciously dive into it and understand the mechanism of its creation that comes from the limited self. One is to understand the essence of the gross-emotional self in order to transcend further in self-perception and experience. This is called evolution, whether it happens through many life experiences in a natural way or by maturity and grace; the process is the same, no matter how it unfolds through the self.

Q: Are you saying that the life-force is not in the tailbone? So, it means that there is no sense in sitting in the lotus pose and trying to meditate but rather, we would be better off just contemplating?

A: What relation does the brain have to our tailbone? When it comes to the physical dimension, everything we are starts and ends in the sacred chamber – in the brain. Our essence however, is subtle. All the digestive, sexual and other glands (in this case the prostate for males and the ovaries for females) are connected and governed by the brain and upper glands. People look at symptoms and feelings in the body and do not realise what the process actually is. Sitting in a particular position contracts or closes a certain flow within the subtle body in order to accentuate the flow in other areas.

True Yoga is hardly known in this day and age, and unfortunately, people only speculate and retell superficial experiences that they associate with Yoga or kundalini awakening. This science will still remain widely unknown to the public for many, many years to come. True Yoga is beyond anything one can imagine in this day and age. When imagination, logic and sensual perception end, True Yoga begins. It is inseparable from Natural Being and living.

Q: I want to awaken and raise my kundalini. How do I do it?

A: Conscious awakening does not entail anything that rises. This idea is only a metaphor. Conscious awakening is still very rare and cannot be bought. One has to be pure and ripened within to contain such an experience. Many spiritual charlatans and magicians disguise themselves as spiritual gurus and givers of shaktipat, or as those who awaken kundalini, when in reality, they only lure people into the world of the occult and entities. That is why so many people think that kundalini awakening leads to psychosis or other such phenomena like possession or subtle body experiences. None of this is true kundalini awakening. True awakening is only for those rare, mature, pure and selfless beings, not for the masses.

Q: Lately, I have been feeling pressure in my head and feel powerful. It feels like I have god-like energy. I am not interested in attaining powers, but can you tell me what may happen during this process?

A: It is very easy to confuse spiritual awakening with spiritual possession. Kundalini awakening is about awakening to one's Ultimate Being – blissful empty awareness. Through this inner connection with the Ultimate, one also activates on the physical level. Just having glandular activation is not kundalini awakening, since the process of spiritual evolution involves the overall expansion of one's awareness – and being in blissful equanimity while refining the self. If one awakens and does not refine or transform the inner conditionings and distortions, then that is not awakening. Having an energy rush or buzz is also not kundalini or spiritual awakening. People use drugs to stimulate various parts of the brain, for example, to get glimpses of the subtler realms and have various hallucinatory experiences, yet there is nothing spiritual or evolutionary about this, only delusion and more confusion.

Q: Does samadhi make everything so slow that even the metabolism and thought processes can be stopped effortlessly? I have fluttering in the chest area, is this a sign of entities leaving me?

A: True spiritual awakening rejuvenates the body. The metabolism improves due to the fact that one has consciously learnt to let go of all the gross-emotional rubbish. One experiences Yoga and samadhi, and from there, the true awakening begins, as one comes to understand what is always present – one's Ultimate Being. One comes to see the transitory states of the self at the same time, and this initiates the process of inner refinement, where one goes through the harsh process of transformation and purgation and learns to simplify one's being and lifestyle. One's perception changes so that the external factors leave less and less of an impression in one's absorbed mind. One's consciousness has to be reflected in the body. This is called integration. If there is no integration, then the process is an incorrect one.

During samadhi, one is absorbed into blissful Being and experiences nothing. Such absorptions are natural and spontaneous for the awakened being. Yet, one needs to master them in order to come out of them properly and function in the world.

The various physical sensations you feel are actually sensations of the subtle body, felt as if they are physical. True awakening is smooth and blissful, and, if any challenges occur, one is able to consciously navigate out of them with guidance. Param-Para is essential for the process, but it is possible only for those mature beings whose consciousness offers them the opportunity to receive such grace of proper guidance. All others wander in the dark.

Q: I have felt many sensations in my body, especially a sense of sexual excitement. Is this normal?

A: You are not experiencing full activation, only vibrations in the lower glands where there is probably a lower form of bliss taking place. All the glands are guided by the upper glands in the head, so a proper and complete activation involving these glands is a must. The activation of the pituitary gland leads to the activation of all the others.

Q: Does kundalini awakening solve all our problems?

A: Kundalini awakening is not for resolving problems but for turning your awareness inwards and making you understand the root causes of your problems, your interpretations of them, and the self-created suffering within. It pushes one to understand that there is no suffering or happiness, but only a constant and neutral flow of life, blissful awareness and equanimity. Our individual consciousness puts a name to the experience rather than flows with the experience without becoming entangled in it.

Through the root of one's being, one understands all that is temporary and transitory so that one's perception refines. Once refined, one flows. When we want to be happy, we have to face all the miseries of the transitory, self-created illusory self. Do not long for happiness, and do not try to resolve suffering. Dive into it all and see how you created it all within the self. This is the path out of duality and into multidimensionality and transcendence.

Q: How do I know if my kundalini is awake?

A: Consciousness is awake when one has experienced the absorbed, equanimous, blissful, space-like Being, as the self, and when one is able to recognise the transitory aspects of the self as being a part of the self but without identifying to it as oneself. Through such Yoga, one is initiated into the process of conscious self-refinement, through which one is able to understand the inner impediments of an emotional nature and to refine them through the blissful Being, seeing oneself as one and as a multidimensional illusion at the same time. Through this guided process, we gradually evolve through eternity, as our body also transforms. This process is called 'spiritual awakening' or 'kundalini awakening' (or something else depending on the tradition). It is the beginning of further conscious evolution.

Q: Can you still have kriyas in a state of absorption?

A: Absorption means inner silence and complete contentment. It is the deep relaxation in the body through which kriyas happen. The deeper you refine, the more silence and bliss prevail in your being.

Q: Can we realise the complete kechari mudra without frenulum surgery, but just by stretching the tongue and doing talabya?

A: True kechari mudra is not about cutting the frenulum but is the most guarded of all basic Siddha practices. All you read in books or hear about is false information and represents mere remnants of this practice. The knowledge of it has to be initiated only by true Siddha Param-Para.

Q: I have been awakened for the last four days and it is exactly as you describe it.

A: Awakening does not guarantee evolution, especially when one is not being guided and is far from realising the essence of the process, and the point of it. Awakening has to lead to bio-spiritual transformation/alchemy, the enhancement of spiritual intelligence, and the realisation of the self beyond the known reality. If simplicity, selflessness and absorption are not present, then there is no evolution of spiritual intelligence, and so the bodily processes do not result in the completion of the alchemy. This is why such a process needs to be scientifically understood, guided, and gradually and properly initiated and experienced.

Q: My kundalini responds heavily to you, but I am in so much pain in my solar plexus. When I try to release it, I get anxiety and panic attacks. The only way I cannot feel this is to focus and put my energy on my pineal gland so that I feel numb to it. How can I release all this from my solar plexus?

A: The notion that 'my kundalini responds heavily' is utter nonsense. Kundalini is related to the bio-spiritual process of conscious awakening and transformation, which is very far from the New Age nonsense being propagated everywhere these days out of ignorance and a lack of deeper understanding.

Most people have no idea what kundalini awakening is. You respond the way you do because you have occult interference in your life, coming from your ancestors and from other personal issues, so you are afflicted and tormented by some form of negative energy. Thus, you are experiencing an exorcising effect. I am telling you this in order for you to be more aware and to help you contemplate on it, rather than have you hallucinate, imagine and project about such things.

True healing comes from a conscious shift and from inner refinement that reflects itself on the body, so that the body gradually enlightens too. One has to realise this whole process before thinking that one can heal others or save the world, for those who have realised it have also realised in the depth of their being that everything is right, and that nothing is to be changed externally since everyone is living the results of their own choices. Wise people choose to bless in silence, and they do not interfere unless there is a genuine request.

Awakening must lead to conscious refinement and inner integration. It is not about the experience of something of a subtle or physical nature. Your subtle body has awakened, but if you do not know how to go further with it, then what is the purpose? One should become more mature and wiser, and one's spiritual intelligence must evolve. If this does not happen, and the process does not result in selflessness, wisdom, truth, and humble spiritual power, then what is the purpose of it all? Even spiritual experience is transitory unless it transcends one's limited-being.

Q: Is kundalini evil?

A: Kundalini is a Sanskrit word for the active aspect of Pure Consciousness, the aspect that manifests our physical, emotional and other realities. You decide whether it is evil or not. Pure Consciousness is always neutral, beyond good and bad. Defining what is good and bad is something that happens when things are distinguished by an intellect subjected to dual-perception, that judges all it perceives. This judge is within us. When we are pure, we do not judge but only perceive. When we are loaded with karma, we see life through the prisms of those karmas and judge things accordingly, manifesting those karmas in the form of life events and through one's feelings and thoughts. If you watch your reactions to people and to events in your life, then you will see how you manifest karma through your inner reactions and through your thoughts. This is neither evil nor good. It is just what life is.

Q: What do your talks have to do with kundalini? They seem to contain just basic therapy talk.

A: If you already know what kundalini awakening is, then why are you searching? If you have expectations that are limited by the scope of your existent bookish knowledge, or by someone else's knowledge, then you are definitely going to be disappointed. All the occult pursuits and New Age spiritual concepts that people claim (out of ignorance) to be kundalini awakening, are unfortunately far from what true conscious spiritual awakening is. If you let go of all your expectations, disappointments, and judgements, and learn to perceive by coming back to your Natural Being unconditionally, then all the rubbish that requires therapy will come to the surface and gradually make you understand the transitory nature of all the superficial stuff in your life that meets your daily expectations but at the same time resists your inner contentment and equanimity.

The process of kundalini awakening (conscious awakening) is about reconnecting your Ultimate Being with the subtle and physical bodies. Such reconnection requires a lot of contemplation, self-observation, and psycho-spiritual therapy, as well as Param-Para and the protection of the guru. Never draw conclusions about any phenomenon after only having seen a glimpse of it. Immerse yourself in the process and find out for yourself. Everything is just an experience, and Being is always there.

Q: Are the experiences of kundalini awakening very intense and related to 'fire' descending from the crown chakra?

A: If you want to evolve, then you should not expect anything, as evolution is spontaneous and unpredictable for the linear way of thinking. If you already know what the teacher should be like, then you will only meet those teachers who match what your limited imagination and projection creates. They may not be exactly what you are looking for, but if you are ready and open, then you might come across something that is significant for your current stage of evolution. To be ready for such a thing, you must be free from expectations based on bookish knowledge, on other people's experiences, dogmas, New Age ideas, fears, and so forth.

To be free means to be in the present, to have a calling and to go towards it. Fear, expectations and attachment only bring misery and create suffering. Try to first become conscious of your own limitations and work with them; this will cultivate honesty and humbleness out of which simplicity and a readiness for the moment of Now will arise. Awakening means to become aware and more conscious of what was previously unseen and to evolve through constant, conscious purification, realisation, and transformation of the various levels of the self.

Q: I feel an intense pressure in my forehead and in my head generally. Is this normal?

A: Have more hot alkaline water or water with lime. The energetic feelings have to be combined with contemplation, self-observation, and with conscious living. If this is not done, then such a method of bathing in these vibrations can cause imbalances and create physical pressure, because the energy is strong and the readiness of the body to assimilate such vibrations is not yet present. Guidance is also important. Spiritual life is one of conscious evolutionary work, for which one needs to have maturity, intelligence and spiritual discrimination.

Q: I think that some part of the kundalini has reached my upper back/neck and has gotten stuck there, and there is a strong pain. Does this mean that I have some kind of blockage or obstacle in this area?

A: When one is exposed to a strong field of spiritual radiation, then one's glands and nervous system react, and there are more sensations felt in the body. The true meaning of 'kundalini rising' means that you become more deeply aware of the self on various gross and subtle levels. The bodily sensations mean that your body and all its systems are awakening to a new way of operating, and this is why true spiritual evolution is a *bio*-spiritual process. Physical phenomena should just be observed, and one should not pay much attention to them. The energy in the body has simply started to circulate more efficiently, so if there are physical issues and stiffness in the body, then there will be pain. Having oil massages, walking, drinking plenty of water, eating wholesome and nourishing foods, as well as having a deep trust in life, will remove such discomfort. Through initiation and awakening, spontaneous kriyas happen, which create a natural movement of the body that corrects the energy and blood circulation.

Q: I experienced spontaneous kundalini awakening almost a year ago, and I have been meditating daily. Lately, I have been hearing and feeling crackling and popping sounds in my forehead region. I have been focusing on my third eye for many months now. Can you explain what is going on?

A: All these phenomena happen because you are awakening to your subtle body. True spiritual/kundalini awakening is primarily an experience of deep stillness, contentment and blissful emptiness, through which one's perception of reality shifts. After this, one needs to cultivate stillness and awareness in order to navigate through life. This is the hardest part.

True awakening has to lead to inner refinement and inner and outer transformation. Most people these days, are incapable of perceiving and experiencing the self in a pure way and thus awakening to the subtle essence. Most have problems with drugs, occult afflictions, and a lot of negativity in their lives, which is rooted in their victimised being.

Q: How can I open my third eye with kundalini energy?

A: Before you intend to open or close anything, you need to experience your Natural Being. And there is nothing to open or to close. One just needs to shift, and to develop inner maturity in order to break through the inner constraints of being. Everything starts from the experience of the Ultimate. After that, one sees all the veils and transitory phenomena. One cannot see these things before this happens. It is all up to grace.

Q: Is it true that one is under a spell when kundalini activates?

A: It is not true that one is under a spell when this happens. Your consciousness awakens and starts to bring you an understanding regarding the roots of your emotions, reactions and life circumstances. Through this, your vision of life gradually changes, and you move towards your true life purpose.

A spell is when consciousness is used to abuse the will of others or to alter the physical reality, usually by beings who are not highly evolved spiritually. By doing this, they bring more karma into their lives and will have to face a lot of issues. The awakening of consciousness through kundalini can bring spiritual upliftment and evolution, but if it is used for the reasons of power and money-making, then it just entangles one in more karma. The only thing of importance to all this is one's intention.

Q: Is it true that many only experience a 'placebo awakening' by trying to manifest shaktipat in their own mind? And doesn't one need to be chosen and awakened by a guru in order to manifest shaktipat and awaken other people's kundalini?

A: True awakening is for pure vessels only. Knowledge is vibration. Yoga and samadhi are the beginning of awakening, and the enlightened body is the fruit. When this is understood, there is no more pursuit of anything. There is only absolute blissful emptiness and self-born knowledge that permeates the entire being and embodiment of that being. This is true Siddha Param-Para, Siddha Kundalini Yoga and the path of awakening. Go beyond words, logic and intellectualisation. Perceive, and you may understand this all.

Q: There are some very wise people in this world; sometimes wiser than they wish to be. Do you think that there are people who have kundalini already awakened without knowing it?

A: Yes. Kundalini awakening can also be triggered spontaneously when one's soul has ripened. The Knowledge has to be supported by inner experience, by bliss, and by true compassion. Kundalini awakening is the evolutionary process that helps one to evolve, although it does not guarantee the perfection of Siddhahood. It all depends on how you go through the process. For some, it takes years; for others, lifetimes. Your current state, how established you are in yourself and how free you are from concepts and projections, is all that matters.

Q: Many people stuck on the path of kundalini awakening do not speak about self-realisation. Can you explain what this means?

A: Kundalini awakening is only a beginning, and it may result in even more entanglement. Most people get karmically tangled and perish on this path. In this day and age, this path is only for the very few, selfless and courageous beings. Most people are misguided and hallucinate about these matters, get possessed by entities, and thereby assume that they have gained true spiritual power or realisation. The true achievement lies in simplicity, selflessness, pure emanation, and the deep understanding of the illusion and reality within the self. Such a power does not teach, heal or demonstrate itself, but silently permeates each cell of the being that emanates and transmits it. Such a being does not practice anything, but is the Yoga, the meditation, and the realisation itself. Such knowledge is self-born. It cannot be copied or replicated. It is self-sustained and self-preserved. It is indeed rare knowledge. Most people think they have experienced awakening, and yet they are deeply engrossed in ignorance and delusion. Only inner purity and selflessness guarantees self-realisation and inner liberation.

Q: *What is the purpose of Rudraksha? Are they not just like all the other spiritual trinkets you speak of?*

A: A single rudraksha bead itself is unique and potent; when in contact with the body it amplifies the radiation of the body and the circulation of the energy within the body. Some yogis, at the beginning of their journey, may use them as a part of the process, but they are not essential. They are not items to worship nor ones that are going to save you, but they do have an effect on the body and the mind (the electro-magnetic field), and they support one through the understanding of one's inner distortions.

There is no healing without realisation. In order to understand how one is able to channel one's own presence and interact with such objects, one first of all has to understand the essence of the Self and the creation/existence. Without this, all such objects are mere trinkets. The Siddha knowledge of rudraksha is very specific and requires a different perspective on reality wherein certain objects that are used, always have a deeper meaning.

The average person cannot understand this, so for the majority, all these objects are trinkets which they are ignorantly empowering within themselves. Instead, they should encourage and empower themselves to see own their distorted obscure perception first, and to see how this perception blurs their vision, keeps them ignorant and eventually drains them. Repeating the actions of yogis who have a different perception does not lead one to the level of those yogis before one's time.

OCCULT AFFLICTIONS, SPIRITUAL CORRUPTION & THE AGE OF DELUSION

Q: I seek nothing but to be a Siddhartha, but I am under loads of auric attacks which makes it hard to advance. What should I do?

A: Why do you seek to become anything? Why become? Perhaps this is the very root of corruption. Those who search to become, never become. Those who are, are just that.

When there is a need to become or to be something or someone, it is a sign of trying to identify with something or to label the self in a certain crystallised way. Draining one's energy and power of consciousness to constantly project the self in this way, inevitably leads to creating an entrance for the parasitic energy. But the presence of such energy (no matter where it came from) is an indication that there was and is something within that hooks to it and propels it. Contemplate on your early childhood traumas, on the ideology coming from your parents, the society, the beliefs that you have taken for a reality and that work in the background of your being. All of these things will be entrances for the negativity because such things are weaknesses, and instead of propelling wholesomeness they propel separation. Dividing the self and creation leads to suffering and illusions.

Awareness is within creative consciousness, so if you direct the conscious flow towards something you will miss out on being able to see the whole picture. Direct your attention and energy cautiously and know that it is a temporary action. Remain within and observe everything selflessly, without comparing it to yourself or by judging, loving or hating it, then you will arrive at the selfless empty Being that is absolutely content. In this Being, there is only Being.

So far, you have experienced attacks from your ego that has attracted or entangled with various beings and people. Thus, there is no clarity. When there is confusion, one becomes easy prey to other energy forms that challenge one's own body through their occupation of it. Own and cherish your body; nourish it with awareness, observe thoughts, and then you will see the clues to the supposed misery and suffering.

Q: I have had an awakening, but so far it has not given me any powers to manifest or an ability to perform miracles. All it has done is open me up to the debris that is inside of me.

A: True power is not found in the manifestation of any limited powers or 'miracles', but in absolute self-awareness, selflessness, deep contentment, wisdom, and in the understanding of reality and of the illusion. You have been searching in the wrong direction. The more you refine yourself, the clearer your vision will be.

Q: I need help with a satanic ritual abuse, hexagramic curse, which was put on me around ten years ago.

A: Cut and sever the cords with any entities that are attached to you. Repent for the previous connections that allowed you to open the doors to such things, and ask yourself what led you to that place. Fast and pray to the higher power to free you from that. Cut all inner ties and contracts you have made with the self.

Try to understand what led you there in the first place. Forgive and let go of traumatic childhood experiences, and observe if you are condemning anything or anyone or have any subtle anger regarding this. Forgive them, free your memory and try to be in the moment of now. Do not constantly think of attacks but think of the higher power. Try not to eat non-vegetarian food, sugar or stimulants.

Try to keep your mind clear, follow discipline and do not indulge in any abusive behaviour patterns or in any stimulants or addictions. Command the spirits to leave. Own and honour your body. Inwardly ask the higher power to help you from within, invoke it and command negativity and evil to flee. See the roots of the negativity within the self and try to let go, surrendering to the higher power and trusting in higher Being. Fight confusion, procrastination, fears and lust, and you will be fine.

Q: If I were to believe or disbelieve in negative entities and black magic, does that mean I am acknowledging the perspective of having power over/power under the victimised mentality? If it is true that there isn't any more powerful force outside of self, then why would I entertain the existence of a negative occult force influencing my auric field?

A: The answer to the first question is yes. Truth is your Ultimate Existence, all the rest is an illusion that has got the better of all of us even though it is self-created. This process started long ago. We are now living through the time of judgment and of manifesting our corruption and falsehood, and this may cause us to be bound more strongly or it may become our path to liberation. All false spirituality reinforces and dwells on people's fear and on their victimised, corrupted perception of self, so that it creates a need for having power outside of themselves. As long as we believe in anything as being more powerful outside of the self, we are doomed. Most people will never come out of this situation, and that is why they hold so strongly onto the religions and false teachings that promise them salvation while giving them even more illusion. This illusion calms them down and entangles them even more, yet they do not see it. This bondage, fear and pain have to become an incentive towards becoming aware and understanding how illusion plays us from within. All magic and occult points out this corruption and thus becomes a means for liberation through self-refinement.

Once you become aware and notice your victimised perspective you are able to make the first step and observe how your emotions and thoughts become the gateway for negative energy and a hook that enables it to manifest in life. If there is a hook within, then any negative wave from outside will find a response – this is the principle of black magic. Thus, black magic, even if sent from outside in the form of jealousy and other negative emotions, will not work unless one has the same hook within onto which this external emotion latches on to. May awareness and clarity prevail.

Q: I was very lucky to be initiated into Siddha Sri Vidya Parampara and am still drawn towards Siddha blessings. Should I get initiated into Kriya Yoga or should I concentrate on Sri Vidya practice? Can you tell me which mantras you would suggest in order to activate rudraksha beads? Do you know an authentic Navapashanam source, as I would use it to heal others and mitigate karma so that I can help others awaken to the higher Self?

A: You are confused, misled and dreaming. Neither you nor those who claim to know Sri Vidya or kriya yoga are aware of your delusion. Playing with mantras and words without having true evolution is like dancing with demons in order to awaken and then realising that you have been sucked dry.

True Navapashanam is available only by grace. One is to earn that privilege through selflessness and purity. Siddha teaching is not available to anyone in this era. Others use vashikaran – they will denude you of your money in your desire for progress. Demonic spirituality is far from true Siddha teaching. Only beings who are worthy in purity happen to come across it and recognise it, and such beings are almost non-existent.

To heal others means to first be able to awaken and free oneself from this global mental asylum. Otherwise, you are dealing with forces that you have no power over or knowledge of how to deal with, and thus, you only entangle the self more with the illusion and self-deception.

Q: A few years ago, I had this intense heat coming from the base of my spine. It was hot and got halfway up my back with intense pain and then fizzled out roughly around the heart chakra. Ever since then, my life seems screwed up.

A: This is a sign of occult affliction and some karmic payback. Such challenges alone push us towards spirituality and inner refinement. If everything was perfect in life, then your evolution would be very slow. Challenges push us to search for the reality and the essence of existence. This does not mean that there is any meaning to anything; it is just that the mind lives its creation – the illusions within the illusion – and eventually understands it. Then, it gradually finds the way to evolve and to fully exit this illusion.

Q: I occasionally experience physical exhaustion. It often seems to happen after a period of some bliss or peace. I often watch transmissions and look at pictures of spiritual teachers. Do you have any advice on this?

A: Try to understand what it is that you are looking for, and what the actual root of your restlessness or spiritual actions are. By connecting to certain beings who you do not know the essence of, and by considering them as teachers, you open up your system to potential occult attacks or energy loss.

Q: If one raises their kundalini through psychedelics but the energy ends up going down – leading to nervous system issues – would it be possible to get it back up? Also, how long does it take for kundalini yoga to raise one's kundalini?

A: Like most people on this planet, you do not seem to understand the science and the process of kundalini awakening. There is a lot of disinformation, misinformation and speculation out there. There is nothing to raise or to press down. Through the use of psychedelics, one is only able to mess up one's life and create openings to the sub-dimensions that are perceived in this dimension as being unified, and this may lead you to being unable to recover while sending you to a mental hospital. Stop imagining, thinking and projecting. Cultivate inner purity, simplicity and selflessness and you might come across the actual science of kundalini awakening and the process in the right time. If the body and consciousness are polluted, one experiences only the pollution and all that which manifests through that pollution and distortion.

Q: Can we evolve through receiving energy transmissions from self-realised mediums?

A: People evolve through awareness, through the evolution of spiritual intelligence, awakening to the Ultimate Being, through their light-essence and through understanding the root of illusion within the self. Our physical body only exists due to our unfortunately veiled and polluted subtle essence, in the same way that our limited mind-consciousness only exists because of our karma. A self-realised being is self-awoken to their subtle Light-Being, and through internal and external refinement, they emanate their own pure Being. A medium is a host to entities that are unknown to them, and these entities are usually from the transitory and/or lower realms.

Q: Is Tarot a part of good Tantra or black Tantra?

A: There is no good or bad Tantra. There is only intention and its result. Tarot is either a form of spiritual action or simply a joke. It is a method where ignorant people think that they can control or know life by reflecting it back from occult objects or people. It is only a reflection of one's own mind at any given point in time. Spiritually evolved beings simply know everything at any point in time and space because they *are* that Space and that Being. The ignorant ones look for the reflection of the self in the splinters of the broken mirror-like reality within themselves, where they mirror their limited being and look for the truth in the transitory fragments and aspects of the manifested reality. Ignorant ones play at spirituality; wise ones enjoy the natural eternal flow of Being in silence and in absolute blissful wholesomeness without the need for any mediums.

Q: What is the best way to remove black magic from oneself?

A: The best way is to become aware and to understand the way victimisation plays you out. Only the gross-emotional reality is subjected to this sort of thing, and it has no effect on the Ultimate Being which is beyond the collective illusion we have been creating and reinforcing for the last cycle, which started over 10,000 years ago. Every tear you shed, and every pain you experience in this day and age – the age of self-corruption, Kali Yuga – either becomes the way to liberation or the way to more victimisation and more bondage. Your thoughts and emotions will give the clue as to which way you are going.

Entities and mediums in this illusory reality affect us through our emotions and thoughts, as well as through the flaws, impediments or distortions in the individual consciousness – the subtle body. Emotions and negative thoughts become the doorways and hooks for such occult manipulation to have effect. The path of purity is the only path to gradual refinement, but the chance of getting tangled by having a strong resistance to it is very high. This is where guidance is required. Nowadays, everyone is afflicted, and this is the result of karmic payback or a certain kind of entanglement, but it is also a way to manifest and see the corruption, and thus is the way to liberation. Everything is as it should be, and everyone gets a chance to understand this at some point in their existence so that they become aware. Awareness is the key!

Q: I find your videos very negative. Try to be more positive, because you are embracing negativity too much.

A: It is easy to deny reality and to choose to live in ignorance, in hope and in a rose-coloured bubble of self-created delusion, or to fall for the plague that is the New Age. When we logically or emotionally evaluate something or someone, we come at it from our personal view that is veiled by these thoughts and emotions and that is incapable of seeing reality as it is. When one perceives existence as it is, beyond good and bad, then one simply sees the tendencies of the current day and age. At some point in evolution, you will be able to come out of this desire to follow the rainbows and the unicorns, miracles and other such solutions, and will be able to refine the self, by first of all embracing the inner corruption and facing all that is within you.

All my videos are only there to raise one's awareness, but as this is not for your current evolutionary level, you may simply pass over it and think of it as someone's madness, negativity and as a wrong way of being. Learn from Time and from Life; they should be your best teachers and wise companions.

Q: Is it because we are about to leave Kali Yuga that we are seeing so much darkness coming to the surface? Even if it is not ending, the opportunity to grow is surely here, right?

A: Do you think that if we left Kali Yuga and made a step towards something else that we would have shed all the illusions? It is going to take thousands of years of dissipation of darkness and ignorance within each and every unit of the collective consciousness before we can correct our trajectory. So far, we cannot even comprehend or imagine what a more advanced era would be like. Change will happen when the tumour of the man-made and human-propelled illusion dissolves, and when we are back in the Natural World, and when all our Natural Being and power of creation within is unfolded so that wisdom, simplicity and organic living is there. What the focus should be on right now is coming back within and understanding our own delusions, distortions and the inclinations that drive one's life. After a long process of refinement, we will see the essence of existence, creation and the self again as one.

Q: I am rather confused about the concepts of Yugas. Some say that we are in Kali Yuga, and some say that we have entered the New Age of Aquarius already and that Satya Yuga has begun. Can you bring some clarity to this?

A: Even if we came out of Kali Yoga, Dwapara Yuga is not any enlightened era. It is the era of the occult and the exploration of the magical and the supernatural. What enlightenment or Golden Age are you expecting? We have just made the first step out of complete ignorance into learning about supernatural phenomena, yet whilst still being extremely ignorant about all of it and the essence of creation. We have no perception of reality and thus are ignorant. Do not think of it. Refine yourself and understand for yourself.

Q: What is the best way to cultivate inner protection from negative energy?

A: Inner purity and selflessness are the best shield. All negativity is born from within. If something from the outside knocks on your door, and there is no response from within, then it will not enter. The more you feel negative waves, the more they allow you to refine the self and to see what else remains unrefined. With wisdom, any phenomenon can be turned into a simple experience of this dual-reality, where one has the chance to transcend the dual-perception and to learn from both extremes to eventually equalise one's being.

Q: For almost two years now I have been experiencing constant sensations and vibrations in the lower part of my body, and I feel these most when I sit or lay down. The doctor does not know what is wrong with me. Lately, it has become so intense that I cannot sleep. I don't know what to do and it is scaring me. My lower back also hurts. Most of the night, I feel like an electrical outlet. This sensation feels orgasmic at times as well. I do not understand why all this energy is mostly trapped around my genital area. Why isn't the kundalini rising? Can you please tell me what is happening?

A: There may be many reasons; many people experience a premature overstimulation of the subtle body that they take for spiritual awakening. The reality of things, however, is quite different. In most cases, it is a sign of an occult (hidden-from-consciousness) activity or an overstimulation of the nervous and glandular systems due to severe occult afflictions, a form of black magic, a generational curse, or even, in some cases, drug-induced (any form of psychedelics) occult activity, or a voluntary 'spiritual' overstimulation of the physical body, the brain and the mind (sleep deprivation, excessive fasting, over-concentration, extreme physical exercises/exertion (all in the name of false voluntary yogas, occult rituals etc.)).

The overstimulation and imbalance of the subtle body may cause issues in the physical body, the reasons of which are hard to identify by doctors and scientists because there is little-to-know understanding of the subtle realms of human existence. What you may be experiencing, and are consciously unaware of, is a form of imbalance or obstruction in the subtle body that creates issues in the physical. True Spirituality is far from New Age ideas, primitive occultism or amateur magic.

Pursue inner purity. In the case of chronic symptoms of inflammation, fatigue, unexplainable anxiety and cravings, one should consider getting tested for hidden infections and STD's, which are especially prevalent in this current day and age of partying, drugs and sexual promiscuity.

If there is any suspicion of occult activity, it is important to be disciplined and to reduce or quit the consumption of sugar-based substances, grains, meat and any stimulants (caffeinated and alcoholic beverages, drugs etc.) as these substances will exacerbate the occult activities and the further imbalances of the subtle and the physical bodies. In all such cases, it is therapeutic to consume a lot of pure water, preferably natural mineral water as well as hot (50 ° C) water, as it will balance one's digestion, initiate the detoxification process, promoting the rejuvenation of the organs and one's overall wellbeing.

Q: I am suffering but I do not think any dark forces can get through my energy field as I meditate, have not had sex for two years, and am doing qigong and everything I can to purify myself. I am seeking the spiritual of this life and I do not understand why anyone would hurt me or could even be powerful enough to come near me.

A: Inner purity and a wholesome sense of the self are more important than external purity, diet or a lack of sexual activity. These things only define who we are up to a certain point. We need to see the inner motives that drive us from within. Your problem lies in a corrupt sense of the self – victimisation. This victimised perspective generates certain waves within your being that allow negative energy to enter and to hook on to you.

Various pains and imbalances within the subtle body are the reasons for inner negativity, and this may provoke more entanglement within and from the outside. People hurt others through the generation of negative, competitive and jealous thoughts. If you are free from them within, then there are no inner links that such waves may hook on to. Any affliction is either a path leading to more bondage and victimisation, or it becomes a path to liberation if one is aware of the phenomenon and recognises it within.

Your spirituality is of action. True spirituality is the awakening to the Ultimate Existence and recognising it as your Being. When this happens there is nothing much to do, as everything will flow out of this Being, and life will be content. Evil is ignorance and comes from within. May clarity and inner purity prevail.

Q: With relation to true spiritual awakening, does it mean that all the people who are speaking about angels, star-seeds, and so on are having false awakenings and hallucinations?

A: People see what they want to see and hear what they want to hear. Living in one's projections and in myths does not mean anything in spiritual terms. Once the individual soul longs for answers through its inner purity and the desire to be genuine, then it receives. This happens because it does not expect, project or create. It is empty and thus, it gets filled in with even more blissful voidness from which comes self-born knowledge.

Q: Is it enough to meditate or contemplate in silence in order to truly awaken? What happens if we meditate with the help of a master's guidance from a CD? Is this also a form of possession?

A: Music and other types of information carry waves. These waves are reflections of the people who created them. If you are welcoming certain waves, then they will affect you. Even if you do not do this but resonate in a similar way internally, you may welcome unwanted waves from the collective being. This being is the sum of all the waves, thought/emotional forms of the current earthly collective existence.

If we connect to something, whether positive or negative, it means that we are resonating with it or that we have to learn something by understanding that thing. True awakening is as rare a thing as finding a diamond in the sand. True awakening happens when inner sincerity, purity and genuine spiritual maturity lead one within. When one's consciousness turns within, it awakens and understands the root. Once the root is known, all other things are seen as transitory, and this initiates the process of self-refinement. This process is tedious and causes the majority of people to continuously fail in their attempts, but some make it and illuminate their being and realise Immortality. This illumination is beyond the earthly understanding of light. The true light is not known, because it is invisible; it is a radiation beyond normal comprehension.

Q: You assume that Yogananda Paramahamsa was experiencing spiritual hallucinations? Some people I know say they channel messages from 'archangels', but my instinct has always been to question what those entities really are.

A: There is no need to live in your imagination and bring unrefined beings into the picture, project holiness onto them, and worship them by projecting one's own power on them and have it reflecting back on the self. Do not put them, or anyone, on a pedestal. You will know who is who and what is what by cultivating stillness and acceptance, and by refining the self through deep absorption.

Assumptions, ideas, and beliefs, are all delusions. When the vessel is not pure and there is no direct experience, then the truth is not perceived. The teaching is either alive or it is dead, and a human is either immortal or dead – draw your own conclusions.

So far, there is no clear science that explains the phenomena of disembodied souls, entities, and various other occult forces. The majority of people who channel are channelling entities, spirits, or something they know not of. Highly evolved beings will not make contact with unrefined and delusional humans, but spirits and entities are very eager to do so and may call themselves anything that you wish them to, depending on your personal beliefs and delusions. These types of people very often become prey for various occult phenomena and end up in delusion, in a mental asylum, or may commit suicide. These beings are only able to connect to people who have a strong inner victimisation and deeply rooted spiritual narcissism that results in a lack of self-confidence and a desire to be something special. It is very dangerous to want to be something special or to want to feel special, as it eventually leads to delusion and imbalance on all levels.

Q: I have been working as a tarot reader, and I try to understand my clients' minds in order to know their true nature. I never make illusory predictions, but I am wondering how to make sure that I do not transfer my own thoughts onto the readings of my clients.

A: Question your motives and work with any reactions that reveal the roots of self-deception. Ask yourself only one question: how clear and pure are you in life? If you were both the teaching and the guidance within and through this form of yours, would you not see that people want corruption? Would you want to make that corruption keep going in people if you could see that your actions are futile? By being a part of what you promote, you tangle with their thoughts and emotions, and instead of keeping your own space of consciousness clear, you pollute it by entangling it with others. You excuse yourself because you think it is a spiritual thing, but all these arts have nothing to do with true spirituality. One can say that these arts are the arts of a kind of 'dark spirituality'. What do you think that your guidance can do for these people? since it cannot do much. People want temporary relief and then they go back home and do nothing about their problems. Unless people understand their deeply-rooted falsehoods, no one can help them or change them. It will be an act of futility.

Question your motives. You are one of the good yet naive souls that are misled by the forces on this planet in this current age. Whatever I say should not matter; what matters is what you feel. All I am expressing here is because you have asked me. When one is the example of the teaching, one vibrates the teaching and being through their presence alone, in silence, or through words that bring natural clarity. When you ask someone to enter stillness, if they have no experience nor any idea of it, then how can they do it? Stillness is a quality of the natural, awakened-to-the-Self mind. If people were able to be That, then would they still need guidance? No – they would perceive clarity and know and see from within and cut through their falsehood.

Giving advice and divination is like trying to navigate through the world of shadows, where we see the reflections of the veils of those who listen and who offer insight without being able to see the next step. When the veils are lifted, there will be freedom and clarity; then the path clears, and contentment will prevail.

Q: I had black magic done on me and my family, and we have been devastated financially and emotionally from this. I fear what will happen to me, so please connect to my energy and help me.

A: The majority of the world is in the same shoes as you. Cultivate purity and stillness, and drop false ambitions and obsessions, and you will see an improvement. Black magic and the occult works through our inner impurities, and it aims at misleading people from the true inner path to the path of illusion and illusory spirituality. Once you understand this, then all the magic disperses because there is nothing within you to support it or to propel it any further. There are no quick fixes, only the tedious work of self-refinement and of uprooting the inner corruption.

Q: Is there any validity to healing systems like Reiki and pranic healing? Is it possible to heal other body-minds through mental intention and giving physical help?

A: When one understands the essence of reality and existence, then there is no healing; there is only existence to which one reconnects, and doing this restores the balance of all the elements of the self. True healing is when one comes back to one's natural, equanimous Being. This is both so simple and so difficult to achieve at the same time for the complex, action-oriented mind. Our limited mind wants action. It does not know the science of being or the science of wellbeing because it lives apart from the natural flow. That is why we have created all these ideas, concepts, and ways of doing, because these things are not a part of an integrated consciousness or realised Being. These things all seem to be different and separate elements of one and the same thing. So, who is healing who? Is a sick person healing another sick person?

Q: Can you explain the difference between spiritual possession and awakening?

A: Many symptoms that people consider to be kundalini awakening symptoms, such as strange and uncontrollable kriyas, speaking in tongues, and so on, are actually signs of possession, where a foreign entity or force is present. True kundalini awakening is extremely rare in this day and age. People stimulate their upper glands, take psychedelics, and do all sorts of spiritual actions and nonsense, and due to their lack of inner purity, when doing this, they push all their karmic baggage and impurities to the surface thinking that this is a sign of awakening. It is only a sign of delusion that may lead them to a mental asylum. True awakening is very smooth, and if there are certain challenges, one will know how to work with and neutralise them through the cultivation of more selflessness and inner purity.

Q: According to astrology, when does the age of ignorance and delusion end, and what is the quality of the age to come?

A: Hopefully people will try to stop the torture and genocide that has been going on for thousands of years and come to a level of more awareness, but there is nothing much that we can expect regarding this. To socially advance takes many thousands of years, as does self-refinement. Corruption takes time to occur, and refining away from it does too. In a spiritual sense, people will still be very much interested in the occult, so they will project true spirituality onto the occult. The occult is nothing but having knowledge about the natural forces of creation. Currently, such knowledge is obscure and ritualistic, and has nothing to do with

79

the real forces of the Natural World. Thus, people who often employ such knowledge publicly and with the intent to resolve issues in people's lives, and who promote themselves through power and money, are corrupt within. Such delusion will prevail for some time, until some pioneers can dissolve such internal misconceptions by having understood the consequences of such an abuse of knowledge and its attendant errors, and thus, they will be able to help the collective evolve. So far, this is a long-term project, and there is no need to entertain thoughts about it.

We are to learn from what is here presently, and cultivate our own purity, awareness and simplicity. Then, perhaps we may or may not be able to make a difference as a pure drop in the collective pollution. Everything depends on the individual and collective will, and in which direction it will be employed.

Q: Are children in particular, and humans in general, inherently healthy and non-violent if they are allowed to be, and if they are nurtured properly?

A: The main question is: who is in that body? If you look deeper, you will understand that just observing the human form is not enough to tell us if we are observing a human being. This may sound harsh because this fact is not yet understood by most. This is the age of darkness, so, many things in this world do not appear as they really are at their core. There are all kinds of souls and entities that incarnate in human form in this time, and many are present in a disembodied state waiting for their time to incarnate. Such beings affect living beings and their choices through the manipulation of their thoughts and emotions, and thus, our experience here becomes distorted on various levels.

80

Spirituality is not a one-sided thing and as humans, we need to be aware of both the obvious phenomena around us as well as the occult phenomena. Only then can we create balanced modes of living and existing. People do not realise that the illusion of over-positivity and one-sided spirituality leads nowhere. Various mental, psychiatric and addiction issues are related to the occult and to spiritual possession and ancestral issues, together with the programs of self-victimisation and the lack of proper nurturing in the family. But all is right for this point in time, for long ago, Siddhas, yogis and other masters predicted that this current cycle of time would come.

Q: Are we in the age of darkness due to the slowing of the Sun's activity, and are we heading for a mini ice age?

A: It is true that there are evolutionary cycles, and the planets and stars are only external indicators of this. The Sun plays an important role in the evolutionary and geophysical cycles of the Earth. The core of the planet and the intensity of gravity and other factors play a certain role in deciding what souls can be hosted on this planet and what experiences these souls and entities will have here. Our current Dark Age means that we are in the age of ignorance where we have an obscured perception of the self and of reality, where information is only conveyed at the level of words, symbols and logic, and thus, is obscured. Our knowledge is incomplete due to our inability to perceive beyond words, thoughts and emotions.

In addition to this, there is a lot of involvement in occult activity going on behind the scenes that people are entangled in in an effort to gain more than this transitory world can actually offer. One eventually pays for this, because by accessing subtler realms, one has to give back in some way at some point in this existence. By being bound to this reality emotionally and mentally, they will have to keep coming back in order to pay off these debts. This current time is the time for paying back these debts, for understanding them, and thus, transcending out of this realm.

These Dark Ages also mean that there are more lower-vibration entities being born in human bodies in order to have an experience on Earth. This means that there is more bestial behaviour and animosity taking place: sexual perversion, tattooing, body augmentation, complete ignorance and superficiality. This is neither good nor bad; it just means that it is part of a certain cycle and evolutionary experience. Everything happens in due time and everything is always correct.

Q: I had an experience where I had a very painful tooth problem that was healed by a man that I met in a Sikh temple. What did that man do to me?

A: Impediments of a physical nature are, in the majority of cases, of a subtle nature, coming from our consciousness. Once one is able to shift or alter those waves of consciousness, healing occurs. The problem with such a 'solution' as you experienced, comes about when one considers who is doing the healing, with which state of consciousness they are doing it, and what medium or entity they are using in order to achieve the healing. The majority of these people use occult means and mediums. When you do such a thing, you may get a 'solution', but you might not be aware of what you are giving in return and how you will need to pay in the long run.

Q: I believe it is common for people to develop a spiritual ego early in their awakening through a lack of knowledge, not through possession as you suggest.

A: Before agreeing or disagreeing with anything, one needs to understand the science of possession and the realm in which it happens, and how and why it affects the physical being. It is not so much about being possessed, as in the case of having psychosis or a mental illness, but more about spiritual occult afflictions, where one remains under the control of a certain source that is usually of a spiritual or subtle nature due to the use of 'spiritual' or other drugs, or through an affliction coming from a guru or an occult representative who does this in the name of spirituality for commercial reasons or in order to suck one's energy, or due to karmic ancestral afflictions, black magic, etc. This world and contemporary spirituality are not a bed of roses, so it is time to take off those rose-coloured glasses.

The phenomenon of vashikaran – the ability to attract in order to control – and other occult and magical sciences put forward in the name of spirituality, unfortunately prevail at this time, and millions fall prey to it. Why does all this happen? Because there is no complete knowledge or awareness of what true spirituality and the spiritual science of evolution is, or knowledge of what we are as human beings and what reality and illusion is. Because of this, there is a lot of room for the speculation, deception and delusion that happens under the name of spiritual enlightenment, liberation and knowledge.

Q: Can you explain what negative entities are? Are they a form of negative energy?

A: Everything resides within us, yet the level of self-awareness defines what we are and how we perceive reality. When our perception is obscure, we see in a way where everything is separate from ourselves. The more we grow in awareness and refine our perception, the more we understand the actual reality with all its phenomena. Our thinking and our emotional reality play a great role in our understanding of various forms of energy and their connection to our individual and collective consciousness. Our current society is deeply victimised and afflicted from within, and that is why we find ourselves entangled in the spirituality of speculation, hallucination and mesmerism, magic and the occult, rather than that of blissful emptiness. Those who want to perceive the truth will eventually perceive it within.

Q: The music you use in one video has Shakti emanating from it. Do you recommend using that music and your own transmissions as a source of Shakti?

A: I do not recommend anyone's music. I recommend inner silence, simplicity and self-refinement through inner observation and humility. Shakti means the power of Consciousness manifesting. Those who are aware of their power of Consciousness and who navigate it with awareness, are masters. All others express their emotions in the range of 'very low' to 'very high' in whatever artistic form they choose or in a game of playing 'spiritual master'. Illusion still permeates this realm of expression since there is no refinement and no deeper awareness happening.

84

These videos are not about any energy boosts, Shakti, or New Age bullshit. They are there to raise one's awareness about the self, and to offer an experience of natural, effortless meditation which leads to absorption and therefore to the awakening of the self. But this alone is not enough, since a deep understanding of the process of awakening and refinement is required, along with close guidance.

True spirituality cannot be understood or experienced by the majority, as the path of facing and refining self is an extremely hard one due to the complexity of the individual mind filled with too much information, emotion, thoughts and karmic impressions. This is also why the majority of people keep on entertaining themselves with spiritual music, binaural beats and empty talks. Transmission has to be pure and come from a refined and selfless self, then transmission truly touches the other and transforms and empowers them to become a better-evolved version of the manifested self. Such a transmission is rare and hard to recognise, only the refined mind can understand such refined transmissions.

Q: All things are created by Jesus, and you are his child, and he loves you. It breaks his heart to see you give yourself to demonic spirits.

A: Discriminating and judging are at the core of all the evil on this Earth. They are the sign of the spiritual ego. The Bible talks a lot about this. When one is in equanimity within, one is above judgement, as one only perceives, flows and emanates the eternal moment of truth. In that moment, one does not discriminate, judge or hurt others. Thus, one remains in truth. Bypass words, for they only delude.

Q: Do chakras exist in the same way that I see them described in many guided meditations? Do you need to open the seven primary energy centres in the body in order to have spiritual growth?

A: Question everything and neither believe nor disbelieve in anything. By accepting someone's concepts blindly, and without having a profound experience of that phenomenon yourself, you become prone to imagining and hallucinating while measuring yourself against and trying to adapt yourself to a certain concept which you apply to yourself. Doing this has led to the New Age plague and its hallucination, where spirituality has become speculation, an act, or an illusion, rather than being.

Q: I am involved in several magical lodges. I am attracting students and have received compliments from authors of occult books and have been asked to contribute to occult journals. I feel that this is a trap and have been questioning my own motives as I try to channel it in the direction of love and service to others. My health is crap; my life is upside down, and yet people call me 'master'.

A: Simplicity, truthfulness to the self, and humbleness are the keys to success. If you see something that is not right, then you should use the power of your Consciousness to change the path you are on or to change the circumstances. The ignorant will praise any trick and call it magic, but those who know do not get involved with such tricks and demonstrations.

Your Consciousness is guiding you, so make sure you have enough will in order to master and recreate your life. Take time for yourself and go into seclusion for a while, otherwise your thoughts and emotions will be taking you deeper into the circle of self-created illusion.

Q: How can anyone even aspire to have faith in your dharma when your perspective on Hindu ('Eastern') dharma is in direct contradiction to the scriptures which promise moksha?

A: Truth is beyond faith or hope. Truth, true knowledge, the Ultimate Reality, are all one and the same thing, and it is self-protected from the projected illusions of the limited human existence.

You say something, but there is no essence behind what you say. It is all theory, and as long as you follow dead theories, hopes and promises, you remain in bondage to those things. If you ever come across a truly free or liberated person, then you will not even have anything to compare that person with except dead, rewritten scriptures that can only become alive once one is alive within.

To be alive within means one has returned to the natural Ultimate Being and that one has seen through the falsehood. By seeing like this, one has refined, and thus one remains untouched by the impure and limited illusionary streams. It also means that one is walking the living path, and that one becomes themselves a scripture and a vessel of knowledge that emanates living eternal Being rather than talks or theorises/speculates about it.

Truth is self-projected, and as long as one is veiled by concepts, ideas, theories and one's own emotions, one cannot aspire for nor recognise truth, because there is no foundation.

Do you think that many returned to the Natural Being, refined the self to the point of moksha and truly evolved in the past several thousand years? Hardly anyone did, as they all had a context for life! Contemplate on this. This is why the world is corrupt to the brim and why barely any truth or light is left in this day and age. If you know of anyone who to your mind, is liberated, then follow them, and best wishes for your current pursuits.

In order to come across anyone who is truly liberated, one's being has to be able to recognise this being through frequency and connect with it. Thus, one has to aim at purity first, not the conditional, selfish and convenient purity, but the genuine and rare one.

If you want to hear about what moksha is, then you may, but the limited perception will not allow you to deeply comprehend it, because all comprehension is based on a bodily idea of existence. Moksha is Death, Death to all illusions. What if you were a particle, what would your existence be like? Would it be up, down, left, right, warm, cold, good, bad, dark or light? It is nothing of this; the particle is free, and you (as you imagine yourself to be now) are not. As long as you waste your energy on intellectualising, you are only draining yourself of vital energy and gliding along the surface of things. If one does not know the depth of the moment, then one knows of nothing that is true. What then is the use of terms and theories?

Liberation from illusions is evolution itself. One should start with the inner perception only. But how can one do this if the mind does not know of one's own essence, if the mind is projected outwards and has not turned within? By turning it within, you awaken and realise its nature and the nature of existence, and that is where one starts from. But it never happens before the time is right and before one's individual consciousness has matured. Before this happens, one is baseless or foundationless, and all that one thinks and knows of is too.

Good luck with dharma, moksha and Hinduism, or with whatever you want to aspire to within your current illusion and with which you currently resonate. That which binds you eventually shows you the path to being liberated from it. This is the key, and it is realised over time. Time is the true guru and the key to liberation.

Q: Why is it written in some scriptures that moksha is only achieved by reading scriptures?

A: Scriptures have undergone changes over time, through rewriting and through the overall level of degradation in human evolution. At first, there was only transmission; then, this was replaced by stories, which were eventually replaced by the written material that we know of today. However, the higher form of teaching remains (accessible for only a rare few, mature ones) through direct transmission. All true knowledge can only be perceived and activated as transmission. All true knowledge is hidden from the majority by the same subtle inaccessibility, and only one's internal readiness and purity may connect one to that knowledge.

Books, words, and stories are like adaptations of the higher knowledge, and they are suitable only for primitive and imaginative minds. The higher the teaching, the more simple and free it is from words. It is presence, Being, emanation, knowing. Truth is devoid of projections or imagination; it is the Reality itself – pure, endless, eternal Now. In this Reality, there is nothing to add or subtract, nothing to debate about or defend, neither in the past nor in the future. It is right here and right now, empty yet wholesome, blissful yet unbound, simple yet omnipresent.

Stop asking, for your asking comes from a conviction that you know and want to prove something. No one is keen to battle, prove, defend or to make a point except yourself. And what are you proving? If you know, enjoy your being and leave it at that.

You are searching, but your search is wrapped up in righteousness and in a certain idea or expectation, and that is why you can only find that which resembles these ideas and expectations. One can only find the truth when one has no idea what truth is and when one holds no expectations or preconceived ideas. Then one is able to perceive the essence without relating it to former knowledge and experience, without mixing it with them. Only then is one able to evolve, and thus pursue and refine all that which can veil one on other levels.

No matter how logically accurate one may describe the truth and the path, everyone fails in doing so because truth is illogical and irrelevant compared to the world of illusions, and thus, it can only be known through pure perception beyond the current limited human existence. It is like trying to explain the path of quantum particles; if one has a narrow vision of one dimension, then one can never track the particle through the multidimensional reality. The same goes for spirituality. If you look for the truth in the past, you fail; if you do so in the future, you fail; if you look for anything, you fail. But once you drop all efforts and remain in your Natural Being, you perceive beyond imagination, rationalisation or former knowledge, and you realise a glimpse of the Ultimate. In order to know this, one needs to live and act through the Ultimate. Then, one is Yoga, Moksha and the Vessel of the Ultimate. Who cares if someone acknowledges it or does not notice it at all? One is the Existence.

Q: Yoga is Hinduism, which is based on false gods which are demons. There is no such thing as 'god consciousness'. These are the lies and deceptions of Satan himself. Jesus Christ always wants us to have total control of our minds, not to blank out or to empty our minds as meditation requires. We are to always be aware of what we are thinking.

A: Taking things literally on whatever religious or spiritual path one is on leads one into a trap. We can only know the truth from within. Retelling and defending the spiritual achievements of other beings does not lead one to the truth. The truth is within and can only be experienced within. Fanaticism is the sign of ignorance, and ignorance is a spiritual disease that entraps one for a long time.

Q: Your insight is invaluable to me, and I owe you an apology for being so sceptical in the beginning. With so much deception around, I was accustomed to looking for 'lies' and the 'evil'.

A: It is 'a must' to be sceptical and to check people out. There is so much falsehood everywhere, and as long as one propels this falsehood within, one cannot cut through it and see who is who and what is what. Only through humility and self-refinement does one learn to trust life and the self as a part of this flow of life. One gradually comes out of this realm of deception into the Natural Being and sees the natural world for what it is. Then, one sees the man-made reality that deceives and that is the tumour within the natural world. Emotional beings cannot see anything beyond emotions, and that is why the man-made illusion is called the emotional reality.

Q: I am a 'black' magician and yet I have never sought to control anyone but myself. I walk this path in order to understand the dark disposition which has permeated my life and to channel the dark aspects of self for the greater good of mankind. I feel this is required of me in this life.

A: Black magic is so called because people, without involving much morality or consciousness, use the energy of the Earth (vital energy) in order to alter the reality of others against their will or to serve themselves. This is like having wisdom without compassion, and such actions can hurt and enslave. If you do not do this, then you are not a black magician but only interested in the occult. Wisdom by itself is not spiritual intelligence. Only wisdom coupled with compassion is spiritual intelligence.

Q: In my early to mid-twenties, I went through kundalini awakening without proper guidance and fell into a lot of the traps you speak of. It got so bad for me that I found myself attached to some very dark spiritual forces and became their puppet.

A: Spirituality is never one-sided. When consciousness awakens to Being, one experiences various extrasensory phenomena, all the distortions and the pleasant spiritual experiences as well. The main thing is to realise that everything is a transitory experience and that only one's blissful conscious Being is always present. Through this Being, we are to recognise what is transitory, and we are to observe our own darkness and our own light, even though Being is beyond both of these concepts. There is nothing that is right or wrong; there is only the experience of life and conscious bliss.

Q: Why do the people of India have an advantage regarding cultivation of the inner life over those who are born in America, for example? There are many people who need to start on the true path based upon the principles you discuss, but does it all have to do with the right time and place in order for this process to flourish?

A: One's intent, vision and level of spiritual maturity counts more than anything else. America and India are both disadvantageous places concerning spirituality. True knowledge is perceived beyond words only by those who are capable of doing so. The rest enjoy wise but bookish talks, spiritual shows, and propaganda of all sorts which nourish their spiritual dreams and hallucinations.

Whether in India, Latin America or anywhere else, the time and space that we are all sharing now is an age of delusion and spiritual hallucination. Nevertheless, the small amount of people who, due to their maturity and their soul's choice came here to realise the Truth at this point in time, will sooner or later come to the possibility of spiritual growth no matter where they are.

The first delusion you need to wipe away is that there is only spirituality in India. India is sunk in delusion, spiritual hypocrisy, occultism and sexual promiscuity. Most of the people who go to

India get enchanted by occultists who call themselves 'babas', 'gurus', etc., and get taken advantage of sexually, financially and energetically. Unfortunately, no one speaks about this. Every delusional Indian, American or European, is fed bookish spiritual knowledge by these proclaimed 'gurus' and have no experience or spiritual insight to see beyond the spiritual tinsel. Hope is what is sold for a high price everywhere.

Q: I had a kundalini awakening some years ago; it felt like my blocked chakras became unblocked. A month or so later, I got a fever of 105 degrees and saw a white light in my solar plexus that started spinning until I threw up. I looked for information about this but have found very little.

A: You are facing some other issues. Interest in the New Age or in spiritual experimentation is not kundalini awakening or Yoga. You need to check for viral infections and for yeast/mould/fungal growth in the body. All of these things you experience have nothing to do with kundalini awakening. Kundalini awakening is primarily a conscious awakening during which there will certainly be metabolic changes, but the truly prepared body of a being who is awakened through Param-Para cannot display such phenomena. Such phenomena are either physical or occult in origin, or both, in addition to probably coming from previously taken stimulants or hallucinogenic drugs.

Unfortunately, true (conscious) kundalini awakening is still an extremely rare thing despite all the proclamations by delusional and false gurus and teachers. The true science is hardly experienced by any, as the path of awakening and enlightenment is only possible for pure and mature souls. Such souls are almost non-existent on this planet. Other ripened souls may get a taste of all this, yet they are unable to come out of the ties of their self-created delusion. In order to come out of such delusion and illusion, one needs to be ready and to have proper guidance, and this is hard to find too. Through inner purity, a clear vision, and grace, one attains such guidance and progresses in life.

Q: What do you think of self-proclaimed avatars? Their followers scare me, as they worship them as though they are gods. Do you have any advice to help someone see the reality and 'awaken'?

A: There are no avatars and no gods. There are only people who can turn their (as we know it to be) average existence into a more highly vibrant self-aware existence, so that from such transformation comes simplicity, truthfulness to the self, and the presence that transforms others in silence or through speech or gaze. It is this Conscious presence that makes any teaching alive. Avatars and such reincarnated beings are simply a part of the spiritual business model. To be a true Human Being is as difficult as it is to be an avatar. Those who follow anything but the self are sheep. Those who find the true path within are Humans.

Q: Is there room for things like tarot after one has completed one's transformation?

A: The various forms of divination are reflections of one's state of mind-consciousness. They are not able to predict anything but only to reflect the potential within one's current being. Some people may find such things useful for self-exploration, but when one's mind is not able to dwell in its own essence, all such activities can only become methods of self-projection which reflect the self, thus misleading and disempowering one.

When one dwells in stillness and equanimity one's mind does not wonder, so that one stops searching and going on ambitious pursuits, and starts cultivating Natural Being, simplicity and selflessness. One then simplifies one's living and starts to see things that are far beyond one's current perception, without the need for any medium or for any spiritual trinkets.

Q: You claim that the first Guru was Adi Guru. You had better check your Hindu history because Dattatreya was the world's first Guru. He is described in the Mahabharata as an exceptional Rishi (sage) with extraordinary insights and knowledge, and who is adored and raised to be a Guru and an Avatar of Vishnu in the Puranas. Dattatreya is stated in these texts to have renounced the world and to have left his home at an early age to lead a monastic life, then becoming the first living Guru in this world.

A: Existence is beyond any limited period in history, beyond the man-made reality and its ideas, beyond its recorded, rewritten and propagated history or religions. As long as one cherishes bookish knowledge and someone else's ideas, and as long as speculation prevails in one's existence, one is not able to become a vessel of the pure self-born knowledge of existence, but rather keeps gliding along the surface, protecting one's self-limiting beliefs, concepts and views. It takes courage to admit this to oneself and to go beyond such a self-defeating viewpoint. Without courage, there is no further evolution, but rather a deeper sinking into the ego-driven reality of spiritual narcissism.

Existence through Time is an immortal guru indeed, and it does not allow anything ignorant or illusive to pass through. This is why even if the path is known, it is known only by selfless purity, and this purity is acquired only by the virtue of emptying the self from all that which is related to one's bodily existence, limited sensory perceptions, and knowledge that would be irrelevant if one was nothing to the world.

Q: Do you know any psychics who can talk to me?

A: You require no psychic. Just gain the courage to face your emotions without associating with them. You are not the emotions, nor the self-pity, nor the fear. Such things are all from self-imposed negativity. Watch your temporary emotions without letting thoughts connect with them, and without acting on them. Just sit and watch, even when it hurts inside, and you will reap the rewards in life that are beyond your expectations.

Q: I think that sickness and psychic possession are very similar things, and that one of nature's functions is to take back the life of the weak who are unable to direct the life force in the way it was intended. This is how nature maintains its law.

A: Our minds feed the illusion by giving it the energy from our emotions and thoughts, and all occult phenomena feed off of this. Your emotions, positivity, negativity, admiration and so forth, are all food for the illusory reality. Your understanding is close to the truth of things. Everyone is rotting from within and no one lives. They think they live, and they think they die, but neither of these things are true, and from these delusions all other delusions arise. We have no idea about the subtle dimensions of the self, and from this ignorance, the wrong ideas about health and wellbeing arise. We create stories and ideas about existence and try to live them, but reality is beyond stories, beyond games, concepts and beyond ideology. We destroy ourselves from within by having too much of a desire for positivity, and this binds us and does not allow us to understand our inner corruption and its occult origins. But hiding away and choosing to be blind to all this only leads us to more challenges. These challenges push that which is hidden and suppressed to rise to the surface. Coming back to your Natural Being is the only act of self-respect and self-love one can achieve in order to restart the process of evolving out of one's current state of corruption.

THE NATURAL FLOW OF CONSCIOUS REALITY, KNOWLEDGE & EVOLUTION

Q: In trying to connect to our 'higher self', what is it that we are actually connecting to, a different kind of self?

A: All of these terms (higher consciousness, etc.) just refer to dimensions of consciousness. The actual Essence is unmanifested awareness, which is unconditional. Yet so far, all we know is the manifested consciousness, the essence of which is the equanimous unconditional Being. It is not any different consciousness; it is just a refined perception of the self. Our Self is multidimensional and can function through duality and through equanimity. Yet, once you are deeply absorbed within, you are just a Natural Being, without thoughts and emotions. You are the Conscious Being.

Q: I am confused about your transmissions; are they guided meditations, and what are you transmitting?

A: True knowledge is always a transmission, and transmission is from the Being. The Self – the Ultimate Being – is not limited by physical space. True spirituality is unknown to the majority of people, and this is why there is so much speculation regarding the 'left' and the 'right', the 'up' and the 'down', chakras, and other such divisions of matter. The truth is beyond matter yet within it as well (like space), and it does not need logical analysis or identification. It requires one to shift or to return to the Ultimate Self-Being, to the original mind, which is conscious, blissfully aware and unlimited. It is easier to do this than you think. Thinking complicates being. If you find inner stillness and cultivate it through equanimity beyond logic and judgement, then you will perceive.

Q: You say that 'True knowledge is never re-told but is self-born.' Can you speak on this?

A: There is no other way. The one who knows from within knows no error. Errors occur through the use of words and the misinterpretation of words and actions. Misinterpretation is born of the inner veiling, which each individual has within themselves. True knowledge is self-protected and born of inner purity, as it unfolds without corruption.

Whatever you watch, hear, or witness, you may understand or misunderstand depending on your level of awareness and self-perception, but true knowledge will never unfold in impure vessels. Thus, no one can cheat when it comes to the Truth, Knowledge-Awareness, Absolute Being. These qualities cannot be affected by ignorance, as they exist eternally. Ignorance is temporary and propelled by individuals, remaining for as long as such individuals wish to propel it.

Reality is so simple, but the human world is complex. Embrace simplicity from within and dwell in stillness. Then, you will understand what is conveyed here.

Q: In some spiritual scriptures, it says that a Self-Realised person who dies and dissolves into the Absolute Brahman no longer exists. Why would we no longer want to exist?

A: We always exist; however, the form of existence may change. Those who can preserve their physical body, at some point transcend the body into a subtler form. Our current experience of the emotional reality does not require or even support the need to retain our form for longer periods of time, though such a thing is definitely possible, especially if it is needed for one's further evolutionary development. In order to have such an experience, one's understanding of the self and of the existence needs to be psychologically and spiritually advanced enough to at least be able to face the passing-away of people and generations, and to face aloneness.

Q: Is it not important for us to 'be in our Knowing', the place where fear does not exist, so that we may then make choices for the greater good?

A: True Awareness is unexpressed. Through contemplation, you can go beyond words and perhaps understand this at some point. The individual awareness – the embodied consciousness – is limited, but the ultimate Awareness is always there as Existence itself. It is without expression. That is why, a person existing as 'individual awareness' (or a consciousness), sees only the limited layers of the manifestation. If fear arises, then one needs to face it and understand its roots. The greatest good is as limited as the greatest bad within the limited human perception. True existence is beyond both of these.

Q: How can we ever be sure about the validity of anything we may think we know about life?

A: When we are in the water, we see only the water. Once we stick our heads out, we see beyond the water but are still in the water. Once we come out of the water and fly above it, we see lakes, rivers, valleys and more. Most of our current spirituality is expressed from two standpoints: in the water, or imagining ourselves being out of the water – or, sticking our head out of the water and believing that we have transcended. In all situations, delusion and speculation prevail, and the truth remains veiled and obscured – limited by the scope of one's logical mind and limited unrefined intelligence. Those who see this, attempt to refine themselves and break through. Time holds the key to everything.

Q: Because the answers one gets always seem to lead to more questions, is everything equally right and wrong from the higher perspective?

A: When the mind is free from questions and answers, it dwells in its natural blissful Being. This Being envelops everything that is known to the gross-emotional reality and beyond. It is energy, information, and more than this too.

The limited mind goes into judgement and notions of right and wrong, so its dilemmas become endless. Awakening means one is able to go back into one's natural mind-consciousness and Being, which is beyond thought, emotion or judgement. It is the thing that is the same for everyone and that is beyond the collective. It appears as if it is empty to the manifested world, yet it is fulfilling and content for itself.

This is the nature of one's Being and is the foundation or root of true spirituality that is beyond names and tags. Once you know the root, the task is to refine all the transitory phenomena, to integrate your individual physical self with the Ultimate Blissful Being and to evolve further.

Q: Sitting is still 'doing' because the body is manifesting, so how can one just 'be' without doing? Will moksha make everything stop?

A: One's inner being can be maintained even through doing. When one is connected with the source, all of one's actions are performed through that Being, which is equanimous and free from uncontrollable emotions and the flow of thought. These thoughts come either from one's past or from one's present surroundings. Once one gains mastery and establishes oneself in the content blissful Being, one then perceives life and acts through inner non-action.

Moksha is the conscious withdrawal from the body once one has achieved a certain level of conscious living. True moksha is when one is able to withdraw within yet is able to see things clearly and act with precision and without emotions or extra thoughts that drain one's energy, because whatever is done, is done through the relaxed being; there is contentment within, and so there is no judgement, no control, and no desire to change, yet one creates change and maintains stillness selflessly without any need to create emotional ripples in the illusory world. Then one's actions will be based on deep wisdom, insight and inner contentment rather than on emotional impulses and erratic thoughts.

Q: What are your views on thought, and its relationship to time?

A: Thought is a wave that originates from the conscious space of existence. Thought produces time. Time exists within the space of consciousness as an idea and is only relevant to the limited existence of gross or subtle forms. Consciousness may exist through various separate realms of time, or time-waves, in the limited sense of existence.

Because this very Consciousness is also conscious light-matter within itself, it produces these waves or realms (and thus, timelines) by vibrating. If it is still, then time subsides and is irrelevant. If it vibrates, then the thought of time appears and exists for as long as a certain cluster of consciousness sustains it within itself.

The thoughts you express are thoughts of a human perspective. Thoughts and emotions are simply waves that are emitted outwards by a limited cluster of consciousness in order to sustain the illusion of the embodied existence and its experiences, nothing more. The way you know Time is only relevant to this human existence. Time, in the way that you do not know it, is relevant to other forms of conscious existence within the wholesomeness of conscious light-matter. Conscious light-matter is not light as you understand it either, within the limited human perception, but it vibrates and subsides within only to start vibrating again. This understanding of vibration, or radiation, is beyond the human perception and cannot be grasped by a limited mind. Once one's consciousness is free from thoughts and emotions and does not support the illusion of the current existence within the self, one is able to perceive reality beyond the notions of the bodily existence, and in that space of reality, Time is simply

Existence, and the idea of measuring it does not arise. This is as simply as it can be expressed.

Perceive the transmission beyond these words, so that you may acquire the experience. If you want to entertain your logic or check previously acquired knowledge or are trying to confirm something, such an approach will offer you an invaluable lesson, which is – do not judge any phenomenon by its appearance. The apparatus of your current judgment is limited to the sensory perception of the limited mind. A snake or a bee would agree with me, and possibly disagree with you.

Q: What is deep absorption?

A: It is when the mind-consciousness is turned and absorbed within. When this is done, the consciously-projected waves of our thoughts and emotions subside, and there is no movement, and so then, the Reality beyond human thoughts and emotions is perceived as the pure intelligent self, with its awareness and knowledge of creation. In deep absorption, we perceive that we are in a human form and that there are other dimensions to our existence.

First, we have to understand that we are corrupted to the point of having created this current man-made illusion that is separate from ourselves, from the direct perception of creation, the natural world, and from all the forces that stand behind it. This is why all our knowledge of nature is very obscure, and why all the knowledge of our mind and body is also very far from reality. Thus, what we think of as spirituality has come to exist so that we can simply return to the point where we can dissolve the self-created illusion and understand the natural world. Further evolutionary levels of spirituality currently remain unknown to the majority of people in this day and age.

Q: In being liberated, through the conscious exit from this physical realm, and evolving further, does the ego or individual consciousness/identity (memory-complex) still exist?

A: The logical mind cannot perceive beyond its veils and contractions. It cannot perceive the Reality and cannot Be it. Why look to the stars and risk stumbling at every rock? We have to understand our own delusional state first and see how it affects our being, our quality of living and our relationships. We need to understand the essence of creation first before we think about our exit from it. Once we refine and transform, our perception and quality of living and being changes. Then, we shall know what the true exit is.

The subtle emanations of the Self and its capabilities are still unknown by the majority, even those who claim to have powers. Such powers are abilities to manipulate the gross-emotional dimension, which tangle unrefined beings even more within this dimension. First, be free from this dimension, and then long for further understanding.

Q: At what stage of one's sadhana can one be free from the cycle of birth and death? Where does karma go, and why do you say that there is no good or bad?

A: We are continuously evolving, and thus, every one of us is an eternal student of existence. There are no stages or cycles, all such concepts are mere theory and imagination. The simple, conscious awareness of Self-Being is always there, so let go of everything you have learnt and simply experience.

After proper awakening, one is able to come out of cycles to evolve further. True kundalini sadhana is life itself. It is spontaneous, and it triggers reactions within us. Through the awakening, one becomes aware and sees all that is not the Self, as the limited and transitory aspects of the self – distortions and conditionings – and refines them.

In the time and space of existence that we are all currently inhabiting, it is of great benefit to notice one's emotional distortions in the form of inner victimisation, and to make an effort to break through them with one's awakened awareness. Karma is the vessel of the self – the body. Through this body, you feel and experience, and you can refine the body too. By refining the distortions of consciousness, the body will gradually refine as well.

Many diseases and misfortunes have an occult origin from some point in this long history of spiritual degradation, where people curse each other, are emotionally negative towards one another, and use occult sciences to hurt or control one another. Under such influences, some people choose to take their own lives, and their disembodied being may trouble their family for a long time thereafter. Many people are not aware of this, or they may refuse to talk about it due to a lack of knowledge of and expertise in this area generally. This is how family lines become diseased, suffer and die. A baby is a being, and even though it is in a small and underdeveloped body, it is still a being with a history that comes from the past.

From a higher perspective, there is neither good nor bad; there is only existence through various forms and emanations. Through our dual human-perspective, we divide everything into good and bad, depending on our background, concepts, beliefs, and experiences in the body. No matter what name and form is there, find your inner being where everything exists.

Q: Is the ego to be dissolved and avoided?

A: The ego is an individual essence of our Being. The closer we are to the Being, the subtler the individual essence becomes. Our perception changes from the 'gross', which is entrapped and wrapped up in uncontrollable emotional reactions, to an evolved and transformed blissful individuality.

This individuality is still an individual essence, although it is transcended, subtler, and on a different level. Once we lose the earthly sense of individuality, we are still an individual, but one with more of a collective and subtler nature. The light-matter becomes subtler and more vibrant, on a level that is not visible for the earthly gross-emotional reality.

Q: How can there be a personal awakening if there is no self?

A: There is an embodiment – karma, and the reason for this karma is in the subtle being – the individual consciousness. Of course, in reality, everything is part of the collective cluster. Once this is understood as it is, one refines oneself and reconnects with the Ultimate. Then, the self evolves into the selfless Being, and thus, with time, dissolves the individual and collective karma-body.

Q: Is it true that siddhas are liberated souls who do not have a body and who, because they have obtained moksha, have destroyed all karmas and do not collect any new ones?

A: There is a lot of misconception as to what karma is and what it means for bio-spiritual evolution. An evolved soul who leaves the physical body remains in a subtler body, in what humans call an 'immortal form'. Yet, many of those souls emanated high spiritual vibrations, created change and promoted the True Science, which is unseparated from spirituality while still in the physical body.

Hardly anyone knows what spirituality is at this time. It is not about what you do but about what you are. It is not about who you worship or curse but about something much more profound, where your body – the vessel of karma – holds the key to your further evolution, both on Earth and beyond.

Q: What is the point of repeating that all of us watching this video (because it is very, very, very rare) are not ready and not able to get this knowledge? Throwing pearls before the pigs? If someone shares something with others who are not ready, I hope they share it so that those others can become ready or learn something. Spreading the information that this knowledge is inaccessible brings me no closer to this knowledge. So, what is the point?

A: The point is leaving behind the ambitions and preconceived expectations about life, leaving the desire to divide life into various opposite currents and then run into extremes, trying to escape from one into the other. The point is to realise the greatness of the Natural World and the Creation and cultivate gratitude and selflessness so that the message which is very, very, very rare and not very clear may become clear from within and be recognised for what it is.

An inability to recognise the essence is based on the immature mind, which is rooted in logical and conceptual thinking and excels in finding flaws in words and the ways they are formed but fails to see or perceive the essence behind words, concepts and patterns of self-expression. Such a mind is called immature and blind. It is not a very rare mind. On the contrary, it is a very, very, very common one. Such minds are typically devoid of this very simple ability to recognise the flow of being, the flow of life, the flow of teaching in a singular flow of existence, without dividing it into this or that. Yet, when the mind is immature, it needs an explanation within its own scope of understanding and maturity level, and such a scope is often limited to very simplified and flattened forms of explanation, where repetition is essential, and logic is necessary. And yet, even this approach may, to some, appear confusing and rather annoying, yet still, the essence is not grasped.

What to do? Nothing. Words without a subtle essence are empty. That is why, those who wish to learn, are to learn to be and to perceive the imperceivable rather than to intellectualise and think about it. When the mind quietens, the Ultimate reveals itself, and that which has been known as very, very rare or hidden manifests.

Q: *What are your thoughts on Prakriti and Purusha?*

A: Where there are thoughts, there is no direct perception of Reality. Prakriti and Purusha are simply the existence, which people then try to interpret with their limited minds, so they create concepts about these things and believe in them. I have no thoughts on anything. Existence is Being. There is nothing to add to it. The more you refine, the more you understand the existence. Then, there will be no thoughts, emotions, judgement, or analysis, but only a pure flow of Knowledge coming from absolute awareness.

Q: For some time now, in absorbed states, I have experienced visual phenomena in my meditation. Are these things just part of some kind of spiritual process that I am not accustomed to?

A: Consciousness experiences itself through various phenomena. It first needs to understand all levels of the illusion before it dissolves this illusion within the self. There can be many experiences of a spiritual nature, or of any other nature, but experience only matters when it is integrated and realised and dissolves into Being. There are no permanent experiences. There is only Being. If an experience is temporary, then it is not Being (even though it flows from Being).

An enlightened consciousness results in an enlightened body, not vice versa. You should have your experience and let go of it, and if you are able to integrate any of that experience into the Self, then you will see that neither the experience nor the manifested self is static, but that both flow out of stillness and into stillness, and that the essence is empty and free from illusion.

Thus, a free being is free from the impression of any experience while still fully being that experience itself. They do not recall or reject experiences but are fully aware of the experience through being the experience. They do not crave or need the

111

experience but have the experience and let it go. Freedom is a free conscious flow of the self into and out of the manifestation.

Q: How did you get the knowledge that you have?

A: Through self-born knowledge. Once one is truly awakened and refined to a certain degree, the knowledge unfolds naturally from within. The more purity there is, the more knowledge there will be, and thus, one becomes Yoga, meditation, tantra and enlightenment. Such knowledge is not outside of one's being, and it should not be pursued by one's ambitious and unrefined mind. If one becomes a pure and selfless vessel, one attains tremendous power and knowledge while remaining selfless and living an ordinary life. Life is the greatest teacher and it is full of opportunities to learn. Knowledge only has a pure form. Thus, it protects itself.

Q: Is absolutely everything an illusion, and is there only blissful nothingness?

A: This understanding is just a foundation for refinement, as without refinement and the integration of one's being into one's actions in life (so that one's actions become natural and refined), there can be no evolution. There must be a deep realisation and an evolution of intelligence reflected in the pure and selfless being and their actions.

True teaching is known from within, and the vessel from which such natural knowledge unfolds, vibrates and feeds one's spiritual essence. Absorption is firstly perceived as a tool for refinement because it reveals all that which is of a distorted nature, as when one perceives the roots of joy and suffering. With more refinement, absorption becomes one's pure Being, and this Being and its action become the very food for existence and for longevity. If one does not refine the self through absorption, then the true teaching and spirituality remain dead for them.

NAVIGATING THROUGH THE DISTORTED
FREQUENCIES OF EMOTIONAL REALITY

Q: I watched your video transmission for the first time two years ago, and since then, I have been on an incredible journey. But even though I feel that yours is the only true teaching, there is still something in the way. I have seen ugly visions in my lower body and cannot stabilise my state of being. What is wrong with me?

A: This path is not about watching videos but about facing the distorted self which does not allow you to perceive Reality at all times beyond thoughts, emotions, and projections. If one does not refine the self, then there is no progress. These transmissions are only here to show you an example of the spontaneous emanation of actual meditative absorption, and to invoke such a state within the viewer. Once one understands this truth, one can see the illusions within the self. If one is not working on refining one's perception and getting rid of the illusions, then one is still enslaved within by one's own impure, limited consciousness.

Never expect miracles from others but embrace and learn from life, as life and time are the best teachers; they show you who is who and what is what. By clashing with the manifestation, we learn about our own limitations and can refine them. When you can do this, you will understand what the true spiritual path is, and it is nothing that you can, so far, imagine or project from your thought.

The majority of people in this age cannot grasp even a tiny bit of the Siddha teaching, and there is almost nothing left of it that is still active. All that which is called or marketed 'Siddha' in this day and age, is only low tantra, occult, and something operated by lower entities. The true Siddha Path is beyond comprehension.

All that people can do presently, is look within and gradually awaken to the Reality. Then, they can cultivate it within through absorption and refine the self. If maturity and refinement are not there, then all the words shared here will be empty and should be ignored.

Q: How do I start to refine the self?
A: By cultivating stillness and simplicity. Discarding thoughts, judgments and ideas is the way to disillusionment and selflessness and thus, to subtle refinement. When you are aware of the reality of the subtle levels of creation, you are more equanimous in your perception of the gross-emotional reality, and so you are then able to break through.

Q: I used to think that I could bypass my pains without ever facing them, but doing this would further suppress them. Instead of only fixing my mind on the positive, I focus on the pain that I carry within and dive into it. I realise that there is much work for me to do in this area...

A: Most of the currently-existing spirituality is occult in nature, whether it is directly visible to us or camouflaged. Thus, it is important to have a genuine understanding of what is what before one dives into anything. Most people are fooled and mesmerised by the occult dressed as spirituality because there is too much pain within them, so spirituality is seen only as a tool for self-healing.

True spirituality is concealed from the mainstream public due to the fact that the majority of people cannot relate to it or recognise it. The majority just glide along the surface of things and get more and more entrapped as they foolishly attempt to find a quick fix or a solution to their pain and suffering. The true path is found in facing all, so that through such effort, one refines and matures, and starts to see and to cut through the bullshit. Over time, one may then be able to recognise the actual path of self-refinement through being in stillness and purity. Then, through the grace that is encouraged by such inner purity, one may be able to continue on the path of natural spirituality and evolution. This grace is defined only by the level of purity and selflessness one has. Nothing else can lead you to or buy you a ticket to heaven.

Q: It says, in Yoga Vasistha, that 'He who constantly listens to this dialogue between Rama and Vasistha, is liberated, whatever the circumstances of his life, and attains knowledge of Brahman'. How can this be?

A: The Hindu concept of moksha (liberation) is not understood by many. What does one liberate oneself from? Through leaving the body but still having all the rubbish of the emotions and past vrittis (disturbances of the mind), one is not able to free oneself. That is why moksha is attained whilst living in the body. This happens only through the inner refinement of the emotional and mental impressions of the mind, which results in the complete bio-spiritual evolution of one's being. Then, when one leaves the body, one will no longer be bound to this gross-emotional reality.

Q: I truly never asked for what has happened to me, but it has happened spontaneously. I thought that watching the transmissions would help balance and guide the process, but it has intensified it to a huge degree.

A: I think you misunderstand the essence of transmission. When people refuse to face what is within them, how can they come to stillness? You need to understand what is at the root of the anxieties and issues that are within you, beyond the external factors. Then you will be able to understand what the obstacles are. In trying to boost what you think of as your 'evolution', you are only stumbling on the very thing that you think will help you progress, because each time you try to move forward, you stumble on the very issues that you are refusing to refine and recognise within. We need to hold onto stillness and to the Ultimate, but how can we do so if we have not awoken to it?

Once we awaken, all we then see is the rubbish that needs to be refined, and if we do not face it, then we are not going to go any further. To face it means to face the pain and frustration from an awakened perspective, without any story, and to see the deep roots of things through contemplation.

Only through inner refinement, which may take years or lifetimes, are we able to understand and come to the true and natural spirituality that is all about coming back to our Natural Being. Transmission is there to remind us of our Natural Being, yet if all the rubbish is still there filling us to the brim, then one needs to deal with that first. Do not watch these transmissions intensely but learn to contemplate and to let go of all that which is the past. Remember that for the majority of the people, true spirituality and awakening are unimaginable.

Q: When I connected with you during a transmission, you became Lakshmi and a lot of energy was moving around you.

A: The point of spiritual awakening is to understand the creative potential of one's being first and see how the illusion works through the mind, and then to deconstruct this and transcend in absorption. There is no need to imagine anything, as logic and imagination mislead one into extremes and judgement. Meditation is just the absorbed, blissful Being, and through this, we are able to refine the self and eventually transcend into selflessness and inner simplicity, understanding the transitory nature of all phenomena from the gross to the subtle. Awakening is not about temporary experiences but about being established in one's Ultimate Being.

Q: Every time I build a golden calf, you come along at the right time to set me straight!

A: This is the way to evolve. Through spiritual discrimination you learn what is transitory and what your true being is – the equanimous Self-Being, which is free from transitory conditionings. If one had not built any golden calf, then how would one know that one had any other state besides the transitory one? By building such delusion and realising that it is transitory, one destroys it, as one disillusions oneself and evolves in self-perception.

Q: After years of meditation and contemplation, I seem to be unable to refine myself or remove constant energetic pains and disturbances within my body. Is there any way you can help me refine or dissolve this problem?

119

A: A lot of it is related to viral infections that have gradually affected the bodily systems and overall function. It has all gradually shaped the character and personality of who you are. It takes time for refinement, and one needs to work on oneself day in and day out. We need to see how our beliefs, ideas about life, and choices shaped us into what we are now. It requires courage to face and to change oneself, and it requires a constant catalyst and years of work to allow one to see these things through one's own effort.

Q: I am proud to be a Sanatana Dharmi by birth. You foreigners are getting its value while being far from the real source.

A: Having bookish knowledge and hiding behind names and labels does not make one a Sanatana Dharmi. Through a deep conscious shift that awakens and gives one the experience of the Ultimate and unconditional selfless Being, one may come closer to understanding the actual meaning of Sanatana Dharma, which is beyond words, labels, and the senseless pride of naming and associating the self with anything, becoming anything or trying to be anything. Once one has realised oneself as the Being and not just a fragment of that Being with a name and a label, then one can get to know it and perceive it beyond words.

If you perceive your distortions and refine them – and dissolve the distortions of judgement and comparison, then the light of the equanimous Being will unfold the pathless path of Sanatana Dharma within you. Look beyond the form in order to perceive the formless!

Q: Almost every aspect in my life tends to get worse and bring more struggle, pressure and discomfort. I have no job, almost no skills, a lot of debts and almost no friends. Getting to know Jivanmukti and reading/listening to her has made my life even more complicated. I cannot flow in life because I question everything. Listening to Jivanmukti feels like there is no benefit in trying to be positive and to aim for positive results, so why change anything? Why is it like this? Is it because of the astrology of this time? Why did I manifest Jivanmukti?

A: You are here because somewhere inside, you want to break through. The question is: what have you contributed to all of this in order to be able to manifest it in your life? How many years have you spent unaware of the chaos in your life to now, suddenly see the reality as not what you would like it to be? What do you want it to be like, and what could you do now to change it? What could you let go of and improve right now? A lot of things.

First of all, clean your clutter, clean your storage areas, and sort things out. See the things that you could give away, sell or donate. Free up your space! Observe your inner feelings while doing this and notice what attachments and what association to the self you have with your old stuff on the emotional and physical levels.

Life is a constant process of acquiring and letting go. When we hold onto something on the subtle or physical levels, we thwart the natural flow of life. When we get fixated on one idea, we are blind to all the other multiple possibilities. Jivanmukti does not say that you need to cultivate a certain attitude to life, but first, to try to accept your current situation, state and environment, and see what you could do about it all instead of getting frustrated with it and feeling again like a victim. Take responsibility for your previous actions and own your current state; then you will be able to see clearly and understand in which direction to move.

So first, create order. Secondly, clean everything. Thirdly, bring balance to your diet and lifestyle. Cook for yourself with joy, without thoughts of 'everything is bad' and without having fears for the future. Try to be there consciously in every moment.

After you have calmed down, understand that you survived until now and that therefore you will continue doing so in the future. The main point is that you do not like the way you have survived and how your situation is now. Make an effort to change. Start by understanding what decisions have led to your current situations. Admit your weaknesses and see what you can learn from the current situation.

Contemplate on what you want and write it down. Then, contemplate again, ask yourself what you could do, how, when and with whom in order to improve the current situation. Write an action plan, step by step. Identify flaws in your current lifestyle, your approach to life, belief system and so on, that are subtly or directly hindering your progress or undermining your primary focus or direction. Observe the self-punishing and self-sabotaging programs and patterns and see how you could overcome them within.

If you feel lazy, then overpower it by getting up and doing things and by adhering to discipline. If you do not know how to get by, then start going around and asking for a job. If you are not confident, then contemplate on your strengths and write them down. Overcome stupor and fear and go and simply say to different businesses that you need work. If you are simple, natural and genuine, then no one will say no. The more you analyse, think, get angry and upset, the farther away you are from the actual and simple action that you need to undertake now.

Your way of thinking and inner perception is the only barrier that thwarts the flow of natural living and being. You have hands and a mouth, so be responsible and use them to your advantage; communicate your needs to the world without analysis and expectations.

Planetary positions help to bring certain karmic knots to the surface at certain moments in time. So for you, this is a moment to either break through, or to keep on living and suffering through the victimised, self-sabotaging, limited being.

If you grasp and follow this advice, then you will be able to sort out everything in your life, be able to change it in no time, and balance and let go of the unnecessary baggage within and without.

Q: I am a loser, but I personally don't mind being one; all I worry about in life is that others see me this way.

A: No one is a loser or a winner. Those who are content within the self and who have a heightened vision of life and can live in a well-balanced way in their everyday lives, are able to enjoy and learn from this life in a harmonious and organic way.

Who are others to say they know what you feel and perceive at every moment in your body? They are only able to live through their own programs, perceptions and reflections of this reality. Your experience of the self is yours alone. If you cultivate inner contentment and emanate it in silence with no ideas of inferiority and superiority, then those who are 'others' will admire you for who you are.

Q: I think that a desire for love is at the root of my restlessness. When love is lacking, I find that I get restless. I think this is why I get attracted to certain spiritual teachers.

A: Love is contentment. Attraction has at its root, distortion and incompleteness. Contemplate on this. Your perception of the self is incomplete and thus pushes you to search for that supposed completeness elsewhere. Inside yourself, you need attention, or you need to feel special because contentment is not there. If you start contemplating in this direction, then you might come to an understanding of the biggest issue and hopefully uproot it.

Q: I am single, and I miss closeness and sexual intimacy. How can I find a girlfriend?

A: When one is desperate, other people feel it. Try to collect this projection of wanting the other back into the self. Learn to, first of all, respect and cherish your Being and your time with yourself. Once you become comfortable and content in it, you may discover the source of true confidence and be able to find another person in your life, not through desperation but through contentment and inner clarity. The more you work on the cultivation of true contentment, the more of a chance you will have to improve your life on all levels.

Q: I have noticed that, since working on the root and heart chakras, my cravings have stopped almost overnight. I can see that a lack of self-love truly is damaging.

A: A lack of healthy self-love comes from victimisation, which prevents one from being able to dwell in the present equanimous moment. Victimisation, through memory, constantly drags one to the past and reinforces past emotions, thoughts and pains. True equanimous blissful Being is free from emotions and thoughts; there is a deep trust and rootedness in the present moment through the awakened absorption. This absorption becomes an anchor and a spiritual foundation that heals, transforms and brings true knowledge beyond bookish knowledge and all sorts of intellectual/conceptual speculation.

Cravings arise from discontentment. When the mind turns within, it awakens and experiences tremendous all-abiding contentment. Then, all the cravings can be consciously controlled and, with time, dissolved.

Q: I feel drained by a person who I feel a deep connection with. However, this person does not defeat me because I am awakened and can replenish myself. I wait for the day when this other person awakens and can restore themselves without drawing off me. I do energy work to restore the balance between us and try not to manipulate the relationship to my advantage, but instead, I try to focus on the unconditional love that I give her. I feel that the veil around her is so thick and that it will take a very long time to clear it.

A: Cultivate inner contentment in silence. The more you think of the draining, the more you empower it within. Why does everything have to be action-driven? 'I do this', 'I don't do that'... Who is doing? – the limited self.

I am afraid your understanding of spirituality at this point is still limited by the bodily existence and you cannot see beyond it. Concentrate only on your own reactions and contemplate the origin of these reactions which possibly come from early childhood. There is an entanglement there which you do not see or refuse to see. In your current state of victimisation, your perspective is that of a superior. Let go of the superiority/inferiority axis and of the victimised perspective. Take responsibility for what you feel and for your own emotions without creating a story and without projecting them outwards. Then, you will perhaps understand the reality of things and stop projecting yourself outwards.

Q: I think I have had a premature awakening and feel that my ego has led me into all sorts of confusion and trouble because of it.

A: Any learning experience is difficult without a clear vision and without having true aspiration in your heart. The most important thing is not what has happened, but what you are now after whatever has happened. If you have learnt something, then that is good. If not, then you should continue to strive in order to discriminate the weeds from the wheat. There is no such thing as a premature awakening. Our limited self is evolving out of the victimisation that is the veil over the self. Our sense of identity or ego is a tool that allows us to be able to sustain our physical life, for us to be able to be embodied and to have our experience through it. The problem arises when we have the cancer of self-victimisation that leads us to the programs of self-punishment, self-pity, and feeling that we are against the world. This is a veil that pulls us into the arena of what we think of as 'suffering' and leads us to having illusions about spirituality, to taking drugs, to being involved with the New Age, and to having misconceptions and misinterpretations of reality so that we mostly feel like victims in the world, in our life, and to everyone else. The goal is to first understand all of this before we aim for the stars.

Q: How can we get rid of the karmic bondages that we have created in our past and present lives?

A: To do this requires a long process that happens once one is awakened and is able to see the falsehood within the self from the awakened absorbed perspective. From that moment on, inner refinement becomes an inevitable process. It takes a different amount of time for each individual embodied consciousness to cut through its inner illusions, self-imposed limitations and victimisation, so that one gradually returns to the Natural Being, which is inseparable from the rest of the manifestation. Self-observation and honesty to oneself are key here, as is the desire to refine the self from one's inner illusions, conceptual rubbish and dogmas. That is why this path is also known as the path of liberation from all that which externally drains one's Natural Being.

It is not the world that we are trying to liberate ourselves from but the corrupt man-made reality through which we have created strong and subtle links and through which our Being, by consciously or unconsciously projecting itself outwardly, drains the very vehicle that it resides in – the body. The body is to be understood as an invaluable tool for evolution rather than something that is to be condemned or victimised or seen as something shameful or unworthy. Having such a limited perspective leads people towards self-deception and self-imposed suffering. Alternately, if one is awakened, one sees the body as the very fruit of, or as an emanation of, their conscious Being.

By refining one's distortions and dissolving one's inner limitations, one refines the body and is able to transform various imbalances in it, so that eventually one comes to observe the rejuvenated, vigorous body as a fruit of one's spiritual process. Therefore, internal or subtle liberation will lead to an enlightened physical body.

Q: I have a history of taking drugs and spending time with people who abuse drugs. I am not quite sure when my kundalini awakening happened, but I know that I am really asking for trouble with drugs, as it makes me hypersensitive to experiences.

A: True spirituality is NEVER related to drugs or to the overstimulation of the nervous system, nor is it related to black magic, low tantra or egoic occult knowledge. True spirituality is like space; it is all over, and yet for a limited restless human mind, it is hard to notice, hard to perceive and understand. Through drugs, one can stimulate or overstimulate one's subtle body and experience its phenomena, yet this has nothing to do with the real awakening. By stimulating the subtle body prematurely whilst not yet having enough spiritual maturity or intelligence/wisdom, or a natural awareness of subtle phenomena through an awakened, refined and integrated perspective, and in not having true guidance, one may end up having a nervous breakdown, or hallucinations and psychotic episodes. One's physical reality may also start becoming momentarily overlapped with the subtle one.

All addictions are based on an inner discontentment that arises from a deeply wounded victimised self. To have the will to come out of this slumber and haze, you need to cultivate your will and your courage, and learn to let go of guilt, shame and other repressed emotions within. The key point here is to understand the phenomenon of addiction and the reasons for it. Look for the reasons in your relationship with your parents and from your experiences in early childhood. Understand that your interpretation of reality through those experiences is limited and obscure, and it is the past that has to simply be gone. The more you re-invoke this path within, the more you victimise yourself and prolong the addiction and the miserable experiences in life.

If you want to heal, take responsibility for all your choices and experiences, and do not blame anyone. Do not try to save others or help them if they do not want it themselves, but focus on the self and try to discipline your life, even if it means breaking away from a dark influence in your life or abandoning the company of people who possibly affect you negatively and stimulate you to continue your addictions. One's mind can break through any addiction and bondage. That which binds us, one day becomes a key to liberation. The more you suffer, the more you may want to break through the bondage, unless you choose to be a victim and pity yourself. The choice is always yours.

Q: I have recurring fearful and anxious dreams about disasters, tsunamis, end-of-world scenarios, missing planes, separation, failing exams and other catastrophes. What do such dreams mean?

A: These dreams definitely indicate inner turmoil, emotional turmoil and imbalance at a lower level. You have to cultivate purity and try to control, not in a violent way, but in a conscious way, your lower nature which is somehow currently in control of your being. All external diseases are only manifestations of internal subtle issues as well. These dreams indicate that the root and self-understanding are imbalanced.

Try to simplify your life and not make a big deal out of what you do spiritually or otherwise. Accept life as an indication and as the best platform for inner work. Cultivate stillness and a higher vibration by reading Siddha writings or *Siddha Param-Para*. Create a certain disciplined routine and do not allow victimised or anxious thoughts to control you, so that you can take over the lower negative nature through the cultivation of selflessness, purity, stillness, discipline and acceptance.

No matter how hard or long the journey may look, we need to take the first step. At the end of the day, we need to rely on ourselves and on our ability to overcome our lower nature within and transform it.

Q: How do I refine? My waves do not dissolve even though I know they are of a distorted nature; they will not let go just by my conscious will alone. They even make me sleepy whenever I am absorbed in stillness. Is this occult in nature?

130

A: Everything is within. If we empower certain waves within, then they will find a way to affect the internal and the external. Everything which is occult (hidden), at some point becomes evident, and so it goes with our distortions. This process is guarded by time, and time reveals it all. Time is the greatest teacher, and no one can escape it as a normal living being. Saturn is the planet that manifests this aspect of teaching through time and makes one receive the revelation of one's own corruption externally.

Be aware, conscious and responsible for all the choices you make. Stop dwelling in the past and hoping for the future. Let go. Your present holds all the clues for your inner liberation from your self-created bondage.

Q: I hear your videos; I watch them, and everything seems perfectly sensible, down to Earth and rooted in realism. However, they provoke a conflict within me and my dreams, hopes, illusions and greatest desires.

A: With time, we learn through life and natural experiences so that we can come back to the Natural Being. Time is the best teacher. Turn within and cultivate inner stillness, contentment and understand the true value of existence as the Self.

True renunciation is not about giving up external objects. It is about consciously dissolving internal connections or links with the external manifestation. The world is neutral as long as we are equanimous and content. It simply exists. Such dissolution within results in the realisation of this neutrality and Natural Being.

Q: I do not want to control a certain person, I just do not want to be near them. It was curious when I first noticed that their presence takes me out of alignment. How can someone block our chakras, our spine or our meditation? I am constantly refining, but never quite get there. I am a Siddha, so my free will is not to see this person again but to continue on my path.

A: Other people reflect you. Balance yourself by drawing boundaries. No one can block anything, but if your thoughts and emotions connect with them and accept their flow, then they may affect you because you have opened yourself up and submitted your will.

You are living in illusion, and this concerns your ideas about spirituality too. You are not free from emotions and thoughts and cannot even navigate through all this debris, so by calling yourself this or that, you are not facing the issue. The problem is not the other person, but what you perceive when facing that person. Reflecting the self brings you back to facing the self, and this is what you are avoiding. This is why you go into the delusional spirituality of chakras, meditations, and so on. You have no idea what true meditation is. Silence yourself and be; then understand Natural Being.

Your situation is a sign of an imbalanced mind and body. If you do not want to see this person, no one can make you see anyone. Your will is under someone's control because you allow this by submitting it to others. You have not faced your inner weaknesses on the emotional and mental levels, so now, these people and situations point out these weaknesses. You choose to be a victim and to again point to the outside world. The problem is within you, and you are to understand the weaknesses and distortions that push you into these situations.

Heal yourself by cultivating stillness and understand that other people are there to help you see yourself. Look only within and only work with your own reactions. There is no other way. Stop speculating. Understand the victim and refine it.

Q: I am feeling negative right now, and it makes me feel like aggressively cursing and lashing out at others.

A: Hypocrisy and rudeness is not honesty, but it might take a long time for you to learn this. Take your Time, as Time is your best teacher. This life experience is going to come back in your memory many times in order to show you all its dimensions. One can manage in life without aggression; after all, aggression comes from inner disappointment and from the self-deception that comes from one's overall victimisation. No one is against you. Try not to project all this onto the world, since it is all you are going to see. May clarity and wisdom prevail in your conscious space of Being.

Q: Why is there an absolute need for refinement? Am I not perfect as I am with the unfoldment of my own self and its longings, desires, and its negative and positive preferences?

A: You are only enough in the intellectual sense. If you perceived the self as being adequate on all levels, then there would be only bliss and contentment and deep absorption – the unobstructed and unveiled perception. What needs refinement is the perception, and so far, it is veiled by emotions, thoughts, stories and projections. That is why there is noise instead of silence.

Q: I still struggle with accepting my inner power, and I cannot seem to break out of my stagnation, so my life is going nowhere as a result. I am also curious as to what your thoughts on astrology are.

A: Victimisation, which is at the core of our current existence, is hard to cure. Take full responsibility for your life and see how it tries to communicate your distortions to you. All you have to do is notice this.

True astrology is non-predictive, and its aim is to reveal one's karmic imprints of past distortions and inclinations so that one is able to understand the ways to change one's inner patterns and to know the exact times when to do so.

The entirety of one's life is a karmic imprint, and only after awakening do we understand the essence of the present moment and start living it. But before this happens, we live unconsciously in the past. After awakening, we live our past consciously and refine ourselves through it. There is no need to overcome anything. You only need to understand the pattern of behaviour and also see internally what it is that is creating the situation. Ask yourself what you have contributed to it all, and contemplate on this. Then, you will see the answer, and from that point on you will start awakening and turning more within. Guidance comes at the time when one is ready.

Q: When I was a child, my instinct was to rely on myself more than to rely on my parents.

A: You should rely on no one but yourself and understand Self-Being as a part of this creation. Others are a part of the creation too, yet you are to work on the self and on your own weaknesses and refine them, only then will you be able to understand the purpose of others in your life and existence. This understanding will be free from judgement and antagonism. Creation is wholesome and so are you.

Q: I have heard you talk about the 9 poisons within. You have mentioned greed, jealousy, comparison and competition. I am curious as to what the other five are. Can you explain?

A: All the poisons come from victimisation, spiritual narcissism and ignorance. The main poisons are:

1. Fear, rigidity and ignorance (overthinking and emotions).

2. Ambitions, desires and obsessions (including spiritual ones) based on the obscure perception of reality and inner victimisation.

3. Seeing everything through one's obscure perspective, craving for false freedom (even spiritual), individuality and escapism (spiritual and otherwise) due to the constant discontentment based on early traumatic experiences or misinterpretations of reality.

4. The inability to take responsibility for one's existence (actions, choices, thoughts, emotions) and comprehend existence as it is, and an inability to let go.

5. The inability to give and receive unconditionally, having too much hope, imagination and projection into the past or future and an inability to remain in simplicity.

Q: What if a baby or a very young child suffers extreme physical abuse – does this arise from imperfections in their light-body? It is hard to comprehend some of the violent abuse that lasts a whole childhood.

A: So far, you see/perceive life in a fragmented way within the existence. From such notions arises inner corruption in your interpretation of the existence and the evolutionary journey. Everyone goes through their own experiences in order to understand their inner corruption and refine it at the right moment in this flow of existence.

If one is deeply victimised, then only through certain traumatic experiences do they either have a chance to see the inner corruption and refine it with time or go even deeper down with it. Nothing is static though, and nothing is permanent. That is why, the yogic way is not to analyse, not to look at other people's gardens and not to project or relate too deeply to something outside of the self, but to dwell in one's own equanimous Being. Yet, this level of existence is still foreign to the majority and thus, can be susceptible to criticism. If one dwells at the core of one's equanimous Being, then one sees that everything that happens or has happened and is going to happen, is right and supports one in one's evolutionary journey. Certainly, such a perspective is beyond the current average human emotionally-and-religiously-burdened perspective on reality, where we are pushed to suffer ourselves and/or for others and are encouraged to hope for the best.

When a person lives in hope, they constantly surrender their will, expecting some other forces to take over and fulfil their wishes without understanding their own responsibility for everything that they live through. In the case of abuse, one may choose to moan and re-empower the pain within the self or refine this pain and move on by looking at it from a different perspective.

Victims are so connected with their pain and victimisation internally that even though it is painful to live with, it becomes even more painful for many to live without it, and so they need to reinforce it on and on. If they did not want this pain, then they would find ways to refine it and let it go and move on in life. Yet, they cannot, and maybe do not want to. They feed on the empathy of others and become the biggest emotional energy vampires and passive narcissists themselves. It is an overall psychological issue that many such individuals have to understand and admit within themselves and seek help for. But where would they look for help? In religious or social institutions that are filled with similarly victimised beings who cannot see further than their own noses and simply feed off the idea that they help others?

There is no selflessness, there is no simplicity, and there is an overall emotional imbalance in every step of current earthly life. Thus, there is no true healing. There is only jumping from one extreme to the other, each time hoping for the best. Welcome to the current human society. Live and learn, become aware, and this way, your own negativity may become the source of gradual transformation.

Q: I am going through extremes as I am addicted to emotions, both positive and negative, and because I do not see it as suffering, I welcome it all.

A: We come here to experience the self through various experiences and to deepen our awareness through the various dimensions of the self within time. The inner duality on the level of perception gives birth to the notions of good and bad, dark and light. The essence is void. Contemplate and embrace the neutral flow within, as that is what absorption into the Ultimate is.

Q: I lost three people close to me and I lived in a state of grief, I was scared and living in fear, and felt lost, but then these dead people came back and started to help me heal so that my life got back on track. Our loved ones do not die!

A: The first step in awakening is to understand the corruption within. This corruption is hard to notice as it is interwoven with our being and our thinking – it is the corruption of the victimised being. Once you learn to notice it and to observe it, you gradually move out of it and see it on all levels, from the gross to the subtle. Having constant awareness of it and not allowing oneself to follow such negative waves takes one out of the false notion of reality (where one is a victim), and into being responsible and aware of the Self-Being. In this way, one evolves naturally through life.

Q: Every time I see an animal suffering, I am filled with sadness, but I now understand that I have to own that pain and dissolve it in the light of silence. But still, my mind thinks of this as a subtle escape from the pain and from helping the animals. How does this 'bringing of suffering back to ourselves' help the world?

A: You have understood that even positive emotions are of an illusory nature, as both good and bad emotions entrap. Stillness, equanimity and contemplating on the transitory nature of all phenomena will make you understand that compassion and the desire to help others against their will, along with interfering in any way in the lives of others, which is not based on wisdom and that is not detached in a healthy way, only leads to entanglements, suffering and to more bondage.

Wise people know that 'everything is always right.' Deal with the waves that arise in the space of your own self only. If you are asked for this help and can render this help, then help selflessly and forget. Uproot victimisation patterns, false ideas and projections, and then you will plunge into the deep stillness of the blissful and empty contented Being.

Q: How does one know the difference between being detached and suppressing one's feelings? Also, the wish to be detached is an attachment in itself, is it not?

A: Suffering comes from the subjective understanding of unpleasant situations, which are indicators of the inner distortions in consciousness that are manifested through the body. Through awakened blissful awareness, we can transform the understanding of 'suffering', 'love', 'compassion' and so forth, into neutrality. Words are only words, but the understanding of the inner distortions and the transformation of the root causes results in a complete spiritual transformation of the body and brings inner freedom – a blissful equanimity beyond anything known so far.

Q: I am pansexual, I love all genders and I was born this way. Is pansexuality wrong?

A: You should start to contemplate on the root causes of inner imbalances, either by yourself or with someone's help, and aim for self-refinement so that the understanding of the inner equanimous Being may arise in you. Once you understand the inner Being and become aware of inner distortions and their root causes as not being you, then you will initiate the process of self-healing towards a balanced and healthy sexuality. This is quite unknown as a subject these days, as all that our society presents as normal is the result of inner corruption, imbalance and distortions within consciousness. There is nothing right or wrong with anything; there is just this time and space and the corruptions that people are sharing. The time we are living in is a time of confusion and misunderstanding of many truths. Sexuality, spirituality, and the true nature of reality are some of these truths.

What you call love is far from what love is; emotional love (passions and desires, etc.) has nothing to do with the actual content Being which is Love and everything in existence. Even positive distortions are still distortions because they are certain inclinations and imbalances towards extremes and do not come from inner contentment. In order to experience what I am saying, one has to dive into unconditional Being and see that this Being has no orientation or inclination but is only pure, blissful, empty awareness of self. Such awareness is able to identify all that which is not itself — all the inner distortions within the self — and will gradually understand their root causes and refine them. It takes time and effort to achieve such a thing.

Q: Why are women losing their femininity and becoming feminists?

A: Women in this day and age do not know the essence and the strength of the true feminine, nor do men know the essence of masculinity. There is gender confusion, and those who go into such extremes impose more delusion onto themselves and onto others. True sensuality and femininity cannot be found on the streets or on television or in magazines. It is as rare as large diamonds.

True femininity is intelligence and the free expression of the self in a wise and responsible way. True masculinity is humility and the desire to improve and refine the self under the guidance of the true feminine. This is why men worship goddesses, as they do not perceive any women who would inspire them and help them to refine themselves and to evolve.

Q: If someone is born as a psychic vampire and is raised by parents who are the same, will that soul ever be able to break free of this or will they always need other humans as an energy source?

A: Spiritual narcissism is all over the place; it is one of the diseases of the age we are living in. One only needs or violates something or someone else when one is discontented. The only way to break through all this is to awaken to the equanimous, content Being of the self. This Being is pure and selfless existence which is beyond human judgement or the division of reality into good or bad. Find this Being by letting go of disturbing reactions, perceptions, and interpretations of reality, and by letting go of the desire to control or to be superior.

Q: You have no practical experience or understanding of kundalini but are only fooling people and making a business out of it.

A: Fools debate. Wise ones dwell in stillness. Rigidity and anger lead one to a delusional perception of reality and to self-proclamation. Those who know, emanate that knowledge, whilst others crow like roosters. Spirituality is an actual and self-born inner science for those who are selfless and mature, so others can only dream about it. Rudeness and anger are signs of a lack of refinement and self-mastery.

Instead of looking into the gardens of others, cultivate your own garden and make it bloom. Once it blooms, everyone will perceive the amazing aroma of your flowers, even from a distance. Until this happens, you must weed your garden and cultivate its soil. Those who know do not fight and curse, as they prefer non-interference. They come from a place of ultimate blissful stillness and from deep contentment. You should learn from the wise ones. One day you will definitely learn what true spiritual awakening is and reach your goal if it is directed by selfless hard work, dedication, and non-violence towards your fellow human beings. When we stare into the mirror, it stares back at us, so look into it with love. Rage, righteousness and envy, age us, but truth makes us immortal. May truth prevail.

Q: Is there any happiness or joy coming in spiritual sadhana?

A: One's understanding of what happiness is, is subjected to one's understanding of what pleasure is. Spiritual evolution happens through the equanimous Being, when one's conditionings have fallen away and one's personality has transcended into this equanimity. Before this happens, the awakened consciousness helps one to see one's conditionings more clearly, and this may not always be a pleasant thing. Once one can cultivate spiritual intelligence and discrimination, one rises beyond the concepts of pleasure and pain and accepts life as a flow that has both dualities within oneself. Most people get trapped through the amplified states of their own conditionings, whether those states are enjoyable or not. This is why hardly anyone is able to evolve without guidance, whether from oneself or from the outside.

Q: What can one do when one is filled with passionate discontentment, angst, and a longing desire to change the nature of the material reality? I have been beating my head against the brick wall that is the self and the reality, and I am not getting anywhere.

A: There is a lot of perversion because of our current understanding of what freedom is, and because we live in this understanding. Most of the false understanding of freedom is based on emotional immaturity coupled with our corrupted society and media propaganda. This mixes together with bottled-up and unexpressed emotions, sexual perversion and escapism, along with an aversion to seeing the self with all its good and bad traits. True freedom comes from the inner contentment that is the fruit of the realisation of the equanimous Being within, which eventually makes one a master over one's immature reactions and emotions, and helps one to grow into an emotionally wise and mature, yet mostly-equanimous being, where no propaganda or dogma from the outside effects one. Such a state of Being does not actively seek to rebel against the system or to create an obvious revolution, since everything is correct as part of the natural cycle of human evolution on Earth. Wise and evolved beings accept all this and transform things from behind the scenes.

Q: What should I do when my feelings are hurt by others close to me? Should I embrace such feelings?

A: It is a fact that the old programs of self-pity, lack of confidence and self-respect sabotage our relationships. Our distorted consciousness allows others to take advantage of us when we lack self-respect and project ourselves and our love outwards. Generate love and respect to yourself, though this does not mean that you should become an egotist, rather, you should become balanced and centred within. Cultivate energy in the body; feed and bath it and bring more awareness to it. This will help maintain balance so that you will feel the body once again. Notice the old patterns and see how they rule over your life. Observe how you want to prove to yourself subconsciously that life sucks, that nothing works, and that all relationships fail. Do not expect failure in life but take time to contemplate and distance yourself from these thoughts in order to restore yourself.

Q: If we think badly of someone, does that person think badly of us?

A: We are living in a man-made emotional illusion. It is made up of a field of collective emotions and thoughts, so we are definitely influencing one another with our personal thoughts and emotions, whether consciously or unconsciously. The fields that people create with their emotions and thoughts will affect the fields of others who interact with them and who are connected with them through thought and emotion. This happens especially with people who are closely related.

The True Reality is beyond thoughts and emotions. It is pure perception and awareness. Until you dispel the illusions within the self, you will be prone to the perception of other beings' waves of consciousness. The waves that these people direct towards you will be affecting your process unless you recognise that these waves are not your own and are coming from a foreign source. Our Being is free from thoughts and emotions. If you are aware and absorbed beyond the self, then you will know that no emotions or thoughts are yours, so you will remain in the Reality without thoughts and emotions but only with pure intelligence and spontaneous knowing. Until you can do this, you will be muddled by other people's projections, ideas, emotions, and so on. This is the man-made reality of the current age we live in. It is like a tumour within the natural world, and it is kept alive and propelled by every being who participates in this process.

Q: Can our heart and navel chakras help tell us the truth about love through the feelings we have in our heart and stomach?

A: The emotion of love is not really love. Space contains all things and yet seems as nothing to our gross-emotional reality. What you feel in your stomach or heart are unrefined emotions from the past that are still creating your present and thus the future. All that we know of presently is still our past. Once we realise this and refine, we no longer react in the same way or interpret reality in the same way. We refine our perception of the self and of the body so that our physical body transforms along with our spiritual essence.

Q: *It is so easy to get lost in projections, but I am starting to see a lot of connections to my inner life. However, I am still wondering where these projections come from?*

A: These projections are the result of inner reactions, and the subconscious emotions (the emotional-drives that we are not yet aware of) uniting with thoughts, circumstances, people, or with good or bad manifestations. The more conscious and aware you become of these inner reactions, and the more you learn with awareness through your current life circumstances, the more you come to realise what these reactions are so that you become responsible for them. When you do this, they will transform and dissolve. Once these reactions have left you, the circumstances and situations that resulted from them cease to exist.

Q: *How can it be that I was thinking that all meditation techniques are for silencing the mind and then a video appeared a few hours later where you were explaining exactly this topic? Also, you say that consciousness knows that we have suffered enough, and that grace comes at this point in time. I think I have suffered enough, but could it be that my consciousness does not agree?*

A: Consciousness is you. It manifests all of your experiences so that you can understand what your distortions and inner corruptions are. This process is not a punishment. Suffering is caused by an assumption about reality that you carry within, because you divide reality into suffering and happiness but only want happiness. Both polarities are illusory and unreal. You should not want happiness or unhappiness. You should want contentment, and you should cultivate it through stillness by withdrawing your conscious power from all the unnecessary elements and phenomena within your reality.

Whatever happens in your life has manifested from within. All the people, issues and situations exist in order to show our limited mind its corruption, nothing more. Life is neutral and equanimous, but our limited and corrupt mind assumes things to be otherwise due to the veiled way that we perceive through our mind-body. One can either let go and shift, or continue in one's agonising race towards unrealistic expressions of being, such as happiness.

Q: It is very difficult to look within when one has been raised with all the guilt that religions impress upon the individual. Does detachment become somewhat easier further along on the path? Can we separate our awareness from the mistakes made by the mind and body?

A: Awareness is there watching; it is neutrality. There are no mistakes of the body or the mind. There are only choices made, either consciously or by following the impetus of the emotions. When we learn to separate their calls, we begin to understand how the mechanism of the body-mind structure works. Then, we are able to base our identity on conscious awareness which deepens with time and with evolution. Eventually, there will be no question of attachment, only of making conscious choices.

Q: Are your energy transmissions supposed to dissolve certain emotions like anger or depression? Are they permanent?

A: The transmissions shift your consciousness so that you can change your outlook and perception of the self. You become a witness of your emotions by watching and accepting them and without being involved in them. In this way, you will gradually transform them and grow spiritually.

All is about Consciousness and You. It is not about anyone else. Do not look for enlightenment in any name or form. Before you get on the path, you need to do the 'dirty laundry' of addressing various karmic impressions such as your fears, your emotions, and the thoughts that arise in your active consciousness, and transform them with awareness by witnessing them and accepting them. This is called spiritual practice. Through such practice, you gradually become more mature so that you attain the sahaj (spontaneous) state of the self. You learn to master this state while integrating it with your body/mind structure in this gross-emotional reality.

Q: Three times, kundalini arose through me; the first two times bringing bliss and the third was utter fear and the annihilation of my ego. All of my negative karmas came together. I went to jail and my family abandoned me. The 'light' is everywhere, but I am still hurt.

A: Come out of victimisation. A family just represents a gathering of people. Start everything anew, and do not cause stagnation in your life by feeling like a victim. Look ahead, not backwards. Nothing is ever permanent or static. It is all just an experience, so let go and move on.

Be open and talk to people the way you want them to talk to you. Do not see the world as a threat and try to escape from it but embrace the experiences and choose your further actions and reactions consciously. Be non-violent and honest, and let go of unnecessary thoughts that cause stagnation and a lack of motivation in you. Do not discriminate against or judge others.

Do the best that you can to improve your life by having an improved inner perception, and do not allow victimisation to get the better of you but observe it and uproot it within yourself. Then you will understand what true spirituality and shakti are. Your efforts in this direction will be your true sadhana. By doing this, you will realise the power of absorption and you will change your karma – the vessel of the body that acts and reacts.

Cultivate inner stillness by letting go of everything that is unnecessary within your mind, and remember that life does not stamp or tag people with roles and attributes, but that people do this to themselves. Live free from such tags and from your past.

Q: I find myself at an impasse. I see the power struggles in this world and the pain and suffering that the world's elites are causing. I see what left-wing politics is doing to the entire western world and it makes me feel afraid and angry, so I am inclined towards the right-wing. On the spiritual level, I understand that this is all just a reflection of my consciousness, but I find it difficult not to take a stand, to choose a side and to defend it. I feel like I am being made to face this conflict inside myself.

A: All of this is a part of the gross-emotional reality that we are trying to evolve out of. It is all correct for this moment of our existence. We are all changing and evolving, so this is why certain older models of living seem to be wrong or to not be working anymore. But each and every situation is the right one, and all the players are there because they are a part of the process of life. Life is simply our cumulative consciousness that is evolving and changing. You should just perceive and learn to observe without judgement. If you try to control, it means that you assume a superior position to others.

Life has its own pace, flow and awareness, so one should let everything go in the way it is going, and if you feel like interfering, then you should take full responsibility for it, and never blame life for being unfair. Everything seems right and fair once we take full responsibility for what we experience, and once we see and observe our own feelings and actions. Observe only what you feel and then transform it rather than pointing fingers at others and judging. Reality is multidimensional and hard to see clearly when one looks at it only from one's subjective perspective.

RECOGNISING THE LIVING TEACHING: MANIFESTING THE TEACHER

Q: What is a spiritual teacher and spiritual teaching?

A: In life, to find, recognise and follow a true teaching is something very rare and rather difficult. To call somebody a teacher means to share the very space of Being with them, which is free from superiority and inferiority, to be as one flow of creation and existence. It also means being or becoming (by refining the self on the gross level) the vessel of the teaching through the cultivation of stillness, selflessness and purity. This means that one's consciousness stops clinging, projecting and imagining, and that it realises the essence of the eternal. Such a realisation leads one to breaking through all the conscious internal constraints of the illusive reality, and to eventually attain to the neutral and empty yet extremely potent, wholesome existence. There is no end to the experience of existence through one's being in various forms.

Q: When does someone who is awakened/enlightened become a 'master'?

A: The master is a constant student. When one does not want to heal, teach or change, and when one is a natural emanation of the self, then one has achieved integration and stillness. Mastery is like evolution; it is constant and ongoing.

Q: How do I distinguish between true and false masters?

A: The signs of a true master are: stillness, selflessness, simplicity, inner and outer purity, lack of aging from the moment they achieved mastery, natural humility, free self-expression, modesty, deep absorption into their being, a powerful spiritual emanation and presence that touches and transforms others, deep serenity, a sharp intellect, wisdom and profound knowledge about many spiritual and scientific subjects, a disease-less state, and a deep unlimited awareness and self-born knowledge. Their presence reveals the essence of others. Those who feel hatred and envy towards that master come to understand that they are full of hatred and envy themselves; those who are full of doubts and questions come to understand the root of their restlessness and doubts; and those who want to cultivate purity and innocence discover a true mother in such a master. May all pure beings be able to come across and recognise a true master.

Q: You said that Siddha teaching is not available to anyone in this era, so how can you claim to be connected with Siddha Param-Para?

A: I do not claim anything. One is either a body of knowledge and Siddha emanation or nothing at all. True knowledge is self-preserving, and it does not unfold in impure or immature vessels. Such vessels, even when close to the teaching, cannot recognise it for what it is.

Many people hallucinate and are in touch with entities, even if those entities call themselves Siddhas, Jesus, Muhammed, or whatever. Can the average person really see what such a being is? They cannot. And that is why true spirituality remains concealed.

Those who truly know Spirituality do not expose themselves as being beyond the superficial mass-hallucinated reality. The teaching itself surpasses the individual being. As long as you look at the body or at concepts, you cannot see who is who and what is what.

There are only droplets of knowledge left, yet even a drop can give birth to a sprout in someone who is a rare, pure and selfless vessel. Such vessels are hard to find. Contemplate and cut through all ideas and questions, and dive into stillness. Then, at some point, you will know what I am referring to here.

Q: Would you say that a siddha is someone like Babaji, like the Magi of olden times, like the Merlins, or like a Christ-like being?

A: A Siddha is a pure selfless being who exists and experiences without being tangled up with the experience. Such a being shines through their refined self and the vessel within which that self is contained – their body. Such a being's body is refined, ageless, and has all the qualities of the refined subtle essence. Thus, such a being in the body may have the semblance of the qualities of the subtle Being, natural abilities that are beyond the gross reality (siddhis). Such a being is still, selfless, simple, pure and wise.

Q: I love you.

A: Cultivate a love towards yourself and empower yourself by cultivating stillness and contentment beyond thoughts and emotional projections. When you empower others, who are in the scope of your consciousness, you disempower yourself and submit your will in the process. The true spiritual path is not about worship, or about following in an ignorantly emotional way, or submitting one's will. The true path is the path of cultivating stillness, of realising the Ultimate, and of expanding awareness about the self, the creation and the existence through self-refinement and disillusionment.

Q: Can love be used in order to merge with the teacher more and more over time until one merges completely?

A: All that which is external is transitory. Look for the formless in the form of a teacher and you will find the eternal limitless self.

Q: All spiritual masters seem to have a unique 'signature' for some reason, but I would have thought that no such signature would be left if they were fully refined. How is this so?

A: Such a signature is a refined or unrefined embodied being or expression. As long as one is in the body, there will be a signature. Having this signature is not a problem. The problem is the entanglements that happen through the signature. As long as we are in the body, no matter how refined, there is always a chance for entanglement, if not on a gross then on a subtle level. Even immortals can get entangled. You project holiness onto mortals, like most beings do. Try to connect with the higher power within by cultivating more humility and purity, then you will not need images and names. Look for the formless within the form. If you are unrefined then all you will see or recognise in the other is that which is unrefined within you.

Q: Can you discuss the effectiveness of remote shaktipat, by which I mean shaktipat transmitted by video, recorded sound, internet sessions, or through photos?

A: There is no issue of it being remote or not remote. True Shaktipat is a presence beyond our understanding of creation. It is everywhere, like space. Knowledge is universal and does not belong to one embodied individual. An individual may awaken through being mature and pure enough to contain that knowledge to the degree of their purity and maturity. With inner refinement, one starts emanating such knowledge effortlessly, and anyone who comes in contact with such a being, is reminded of their Natural Being; and they turn within and may awaken too.

True masters do not want you to follow them; they simply emanate selflessness, and you start following yourself by cultivating your own purity and selflessness within. True masters never take credit for the knowledge you experience; they reconnect you with the Ultimate and support you in realising your own truth that empowers your being and furthers your evolution.

Q: Why do some supposedly advanced people talk about being in the void, when it seems that their willpower has been erased to the point of no longer being able to even walk or care for themselves?

A: People talk about all sorts of things; they imagine, and they dream. They cannot accept life for what it is, and so they try to escape. Thus, they can never understand Existence. Some understand elements of the creation but not of the Existence. As long as you are trying to fill your mind with all sorts of rubbish and other people's experiences, how can you restore your Natural Being – the natural mind, the selfless perception?

The system is overloaded. Empty it, purify, and let go. Many people are stuck in bliss like addicts who are also stuck with a good feeling. The point of evolution is far beyond this. Bliss is only the beginning, and at some point, if it is not properly understood or integrated, it turns out to be a spiritual trap. Many people make a big deal out of it and think that they are advanced, evolved, or masters because of it. True masters are like gems; they lay humbly and are unnoticed. Truth is self-protected and remains hidden. It only unfolds naturally in pure, selfless vessels.

Q: There were many shaktipat gurus who, despite their advanced stage, seemed to die an ordinary death. How is this so? Did they reach mahasamadhi?

A: It depends on what you mean by 'shaktipat gurus'? Do you mean self-proclaimed, unrefined beings and those who follow low tantra and the path of vashikaran? In spirituality, there are only two ways to go – either death or immortality. Immortality is very hard to achieve in this day and age. Many people perish due to their inability to refine themselves. To receive true guidance, one needs to evolve to that point of self-refinement and be eligible for it from within. Purity and selflessness are the keys here. And who defines what 'advancement' is? Idiots and spiritual fools? People who know of immortality are hardly known in this day and age.

Q: How does the Siddha Guru remove karma from shishyas?

A: No one is able to remove karma. Only if your awareness rises will you be able to gradually refine yourself and therefore remove karma. This means that your light-body takes over the physical one so that you gradually evolve out of this dimension of life. Then, the physical body dissolves into light. To get to this stage is a very rare level to reach in this day and age.

Q: Will I ever find a guru, and how can I join any spiritual paths without money?

A: The only way to get closer to the path is by the cultivation of inner purity that results in inner spiritual depth – simplicity, contentment, selflessness. This alone makes one come across and recognise a true Siddha guru. The ambition to pursue spirituality without inner contentment and purity is like gliding along the surface of the water without knowing its depth.

For truly pure beings, the teaching is always free. For the rest, it is a path of gratitude, humility and cultivation of selflessness first, before they are truly ready to recognise the teaching within and without and experience it.

'Free' does not relate only to money. Your perception is obscured. That is why you glide along the surface instead of cultivating stillness and contentment in every moment of your existence. That is why you are incapable of recognising the true teaching even when you receive it.

All these people you consider as gurus are people who have not realised the path, neither have they come closer to it, because there is no refinement or realisation within. Rather, they glide along the surface, greedy for recognition and money. Many are just occultists in the most amateur sense. As long as you are gliding along the surface, you will attract those who glide along the surface too. True knowledge needs to be earned by inner purity and selflessness.

Q: The best gurus speak simple words and accept you for what you are; you can see love in their eyes, acceptance and tranquillity in their posture. I met one such man, or rather, he found me. He told me stuff I never wanted to hear, things that, at that time, were repulsive to me (it was too simple for my complicated mind). They can show you how to liberate yourself, but they have no expectations as to whether you will or how long it will take. To them, you are not a failure, you are simply on your path and they are in your life and that is all.

A: Life is neutral. There is neither suffering in it nor happiness; it is existence through creation or beyond creation. So far, everything we experience is within the human context, within the context of creation. As long as one is victimised and projects one's own power outwards, one is not eligible for true knowledge. True knowledge is self-protected and unfolds naturally only within pure vessels who have restored their Natural Being.

People do not understand who is who and what is what. They dream and imagine, create myths and fairy tales, and then believe in them and preach them to others. In this day and age, true knowledge is extremely rare, and one cannot simply understand it. Only because one's mind is impure and does not perceive its Natural Being or dwell in it, does reality remain hidden. People think that they practice or pursue spirituality when in fact, all they do is just engage in spiritual action or cultivate spiritual ambitions, without ever being able to realise the essence. The essence is always there, but busy minds cannot register it.

If Stillness becomes your first teacher and purity is restored, you will come to know what is true and what is false, and only then the physical master will manifest, or you will learn mastery and humility within yourself and continue your evolution further.

Q: For me, kundalini is the most wonderful energy I have ever encountered in my life! Also, I have heard that water retains information, so what happens if we put a picture of a master under the water we drink?

A: Water, and anything with a crystalline structure, retains information. The True Master is within you, and you are within the Master. If you created such a powerful master, then who must you be?

The key is to go within and observe oneself and one's own actions and reactions and to understand illusion and falsehood within the self. Once we understand this, we are able to see the reasons behind us manifesting this falsehood externally in the form of abuse, suffering, false misleading teachings, dogmas, ideas, concepts, and teachers.

Kundalini awakening is conscious awakening to the Ultimate Being which helps one understand the illusion within and thus refine and liberate oneself from it. There is nothing more to it, and everything else is just one's delusion.

True masters are very, very rare, and while some knowledge is true, everything has to be transmitted in order to be understood within the recipient, as words will always mislead. If you tune into and perceive beyond these words, then you will understand much more. As long as your mind wants to question and to receive logical answers, you will want to entertain your intellect, and thus, you are not ripe for true knowledge in the form of transmission. As long as you entertain illusions, how will the reality manifest itself? After you stop reading this, perceive.

Q: What is the difference between being around the enlightened master and spiritual possession? What is the difference between the kinds of transmissions received from an enlightened person and spiritual possession?

A: Enlightened masters do not do anything. They do not give shaktipat. Shaktipat cannot be given, rather, 'giving shaktipat' is the task of unrefined beings, those who give and take, assume roles, positions and superiority. An enlightened master emanates their being as the rose naturally emanates its aroma. Such an emanation is a powerful spiritual field, in which, if one comes to it, one can experience a conscious shift, natural refinement, and stillness. In such a presence, there is no intent.

Occultists, magicians and pseudo-gurus use intent, and that is why there is a level of distance, superiority, labels and charisma created by these beings through the means of occult ritual. Such a presence pulls one, as if, into a bog. Such beings work with entities and occult forces to enhance their presence on the spiritual market, to attract more people and then use the emotional energy of such beings. They are spiritual predators. Those who fall for such phenomena have something within resembling the opposite to what these predators have – victimisation, low self-esteem, the desire for power and siddhis, etc. Thus, everything is right and as it should be in such a situation.

Q: Is it correct that a sadhaka is like a disciple and that a follower is like a student?

A: Sadhaka means practitioner. Shishya means disciple, and chela means follower. Many people are followers, whereas true students are as rare as true teachers. A student is someone worthy of a teacher. All the rest are practitioners and followers.

Q: I am constantly thinking about Sadhguru Jaggi Vasudev.

A: Sadhguru is the unconditional Being – the true reality. What is the point of thinking about it? When you think of something, it is not Sadhguru, but a product of your imagination. In order to realise the Being, let go of all involvement with the mind-consciousness and cultivate natural stillness. Natural stillness leads to natural absorption, and natural absorption leads to self-refinement. Complete refinement leads to inner maturity, and inner maturity leads to a profound expansion, humility, selflessness and simplicity – and it is there that one finds the true Sadhguru. Anything else is just man-made phenomena, and thus an illusion, a delusion, and a product of one's impurities. In order to experience the true Sadhguru, refine yourself, become selfless, and realise the unconditional reality of Being and existence first.

Q: I wonder if I am on the right path. I think I need someone to guide me through the storm.

A: The path is within. It is a pathless path. This path is one's individual journey. Only by grace and by one's own spiritual and emotional maturity is one able to manifest and recognise true guidance that is external. Consciousness knows the right time for this to happen, one always knows within. Take your time and trust in the flow within, for that is life.

Q: Is it impossible to relay spirituality verbally?

A: Words always fail spirituality and spirituality fails words. Inner processes, torments and havoc are hard things to explain verbally as they can only be felt. Psychology tries to get a hold on this, but as with any science that is based on logic, assumption and verbal explanations, it fails. No matter how well we express ourselves or express spiritual concepts in words, there will still be something left that is between the words and that is simply felt and known in silence. Real communication is non-verbal. One day we shall all agree on this point.

Q: Is your book written for people who know what is written in it without having to read it, because your experiences are the same as the readers? And does this then trigger awakening?

A: The experience is manifested when there is a predisposition and receptivity coming from within oneself towards that experience. If one is ready, knowledge manifests and unfolds from within, but only to the degree of one's purity. The more one refines oneself, the deeper one realises this knowledge so that one grasps spirituality in a simpler way. Because spirituality is not separate from one's being, one becomes the vessel of Yoga, meditation and self-born knowledge.

Q: I have let all of my masters down.

A: No one can let a true master down. The true master bathes in blissful emptiness, and is content and selfless, in the ever-eternal Now. This Now is ever pure and free from time, projections and judgment.

Q: I attended a yoga centre some years ago. On the surface, they were super-positive, but unfortunately it turned out to all be a lie.

A: In this day and age, truth remains hidden and reveals itself only to pure selfless beings, if indeed there are such beings still existing on Earth. There is nothing to be found in yoga centres, ashrams or in spiritual beggars posing as spiritual kings.

True mastery lays within one's own ability to understand the essence of each present moment, to reconnect with the natural mind, and to gradually realise the truth within. The true master will always appear once one's being is pure enough to contain higher knowledge. Thus, one should only learn to appreciate existence and let go of all that which tarnishes one's being.

Q: Is true awakening possible for someone who completely surrenders himself to his Master?

A: Yes; if you are connected with the inner flow within, then eventually, through this flow, you will come to realise that *it* is the true master. The actual teacher is always our life, and it teaches through our interaction with different people and circumstances. True surrender means to surrender to that inner content equanimous Being that is present at all times. If you are connected with That, then you are truly able to recognise a true master, a true teaching and a Being as one flow of existence. When this happens, why not surrender to it?

Surrender means that you are conscious, responsible, and content, like stillness itself, at all times. Then, there is no difference between you and a true master. At that point, the seed of self-born knowledge may start unfolding within, because there is purity and because the flow of Self-Being is now unconditional. If one is not mature or selfless, honest and free in expression, then one cannot know the flow and thus, cannot know the Self, Truth, the Reality, the Existence. All these terms mean one and the same thing.

Q: If a teacher has a powerful energy that naturally radiates from them and feels very enlightened, does this mean that I should trust them?

A: You are living in an age of deception and dark forces that operate through people's ignorance and unawareness of the subtler layers of existence, through their greed, envy, fears and victimisation. A truly powerful aura must be humble, like existence itself, where it is always present but does not call attention to itself. The more powerful the being, the more humble, simple and still they are. Light is not a sign of enlightenment, as dark realms can manifest light to deceive people and mislead them with it, making them believe that they are powerful and have achievement. True light is a spiritual radiation that is invisible and selfless. True spiritual radiation is so powerful that no corruption or falsehood can stand it. Such a presence is soothing and absolutely humble, though free from superiority and the desire to be something.

Trust inner stillness, selflessness and life, for it shows you reflections of your own falsehoods and helps you to understand those things if you are willing to. True guidance appears when one is mature and pure enough to trust oneself and see through one's own falsehood.

Q: For years I thought that I had to 'do' and to 'believe' certain things in order to be free, but now I understand from listening to you, that I do not have to do any of those things. But I am aware that I need guidance, so do you have any suggestions as to how to move forward?

A: When one is ripe within, one may come across a teaching, but to recognise that teaching and to live it is a much harder thing to do, and this is why there are so few who receive true guidance. The majority of people only want their narcissism stroked, to hear words of praise, and have their over-blown desire for positivity validated, so they fall prey to the false, lower realm magicians, the dark forces in the form of tantriks and sorcerers who use the seeker's energies and naivety to propel their own dark plans for superiority, money and fame, self-gratification and power. The power of the darker forces is limited though, and is only brought forth by the minds of humanity in its current state. Before someone wants spirituality, they have to become aware of all this before they throw themselves into anything that goes by the name of their spiritual beliefs and delusions. The majority want to touch the stars, to be something, to gain something, and yet they are blind to the dirt that is on their feet and the veils that are in front of their eyes. So, they stumble around and keep on searching, when in reality there is nothing to look for but to go within and be. This is why such people fall for dark spirituality.

True spirituality has no ambition, no greed, no comparison, no competition, and no desires to become or to undo anything in life. Such a path cannot be comprehended by greedy, degraded and ambitious human minds. True spirituality always remains a humble witness to all of this spiritual masquerading.

Q: You are a teacher, but I feel like you are a guru, correct?

A: There are many teachers but hardly any gurus, just as there are many followers but hardly any students. The quality of a student defines the guru, and this is why gurus take a very long time to identify anyone as being more than a follower and call them a student. This means that a student has become worthy of the guru, and it is a very rare phenomenon. If it happens, it means that the guru has found someone equal to themselves in capacity and maturity, someone who can preserve the knowledge of Param-Para. In the space of the Ultimate Being, there is no separation between a guru and an adept because both have dissolved into the same Being.

True gurus and true students are tested and moulded over time, and so it is that a true guru evolves into one only by acquiring the attitude of being an eternal student of life. Through selflessness and humble being, one eventually evolves to the point of being beyond having any need to be called anything or to be acknowledged in any way by anyone. One simply dwells in the contentment of the Self-Being, in blissful, eternal nothingness.

Q: Is it a matter of trial and error, or is it god's will for a genuine seeker to find their guru?

A: It is a must to have inner maturity, inner purity and grace, as well as to have freedom from expectations and projections as to what and how the guru is to be and is to look like. Deep devotional and unconditional love and trust in life unfolds into true and unconditional guidance through the appearance of the true selfless guru.

Guru is the unconditional presence, knowledge beyond words, overall protection, and one's inner core. There is no difference between the self and the guru in the space of the blissful Being, and there cannot be a distance in power between a true guru and a true disciple. It is hardly possible to find and recognise a true guru, and it is even harder to come across a genuine disciple. A true disciple will definitely come across a true guru; the recognition of one another will be instantaneous and beyond logic. Sometimes however, it will take time to understand who is who, so one will learn this only after some time. Everything comes at the right time, and everything is always right.

Q: In your book, you say that the body of the true spiritual adept is slender and that the teacher who has a big belly has an overinflated ego. Can you clarify this?

A: Not everyone that we know of as a 'spiritual' or 'enlightened' being is necessarily a spiritually advanced being. They may not have managed to break through their illusions and emotional reality after awakening, and may not have their advances through the transformation of their body. The body is simply a reflection of who is within the body.

Q: For me, proper guidance on the path has been hard to come by, both practically and spiritually. My awakening was involuntary, and I was left to fend for myself.

A: Proper guidance is always there. While one evolves, one does not stop eating or going to the toilet. The law of sustaining life while evolving is the law of nature, and without an appreciation of this, there can be no gratitude and trust in life. In order to have guidance, there has to be an aspiration and a clear vision, as well as a desire to evolve and to see everything beyond one's victimisation.

Q: Does being exposed to your vibrations have an effect on the people around me?

A: The vibrations you perceive are there in order to bring out the distortions in consciousness. When this happens, there may sometimes be deeper, more hidden layers of negativity that come to the surface and that need to be properly understood. The vibrations are not of a negative nature, but if negativity is present, then such vibrations will push it up to the surface and make one aware of its presence. Such vibrations bring about evolution and change, and sometimes, during these changes, we see no clear path and so we feel as if we are lost within these emotional distortions. Guidance is needed in order to navigate our way out of this.

When the veil is removed and understood, the path is cleared, and we are ready to walk on it and face other distortions within our consciousness that make up our individual emotional self. Thus continues our evolution. This evolution means going beyond positive and negative, beyond the individual into the collective and beyond the collective, where both currents are accepted within the self and explored and neutralised through the equanimous blissful Being.

Q: Can you please make a rare and powerful transmission for the pc muscle, perineum and for the root chakra?

A: Everyone is to go through their life experiences, and they are to understand the root causes of their problems themselves. Do not look for quick fixes or spiritual crutches, for you will only entangle with the illusion more. Observe yourself and refine yourself, see your shortcomings and inclinations, the emotions, concepts and stories that drive your life, instead of looking for someone else to solve your life for you.

This life is for seeing all that is within you, so do not empower others but see the true power and essence of others only when you are mature and empowered within yourself. True power is not superior; it is there as a Being, so turn the mind within and experience that Being. Through this Being you refine yourself. Once you have matured you will know how to proceed further.

True Siddhas do not interfere with other people's lives or wills, because they can see the reasons for other peoples' sufferings. Nor do they accept the ignorant submission of the self. Do not fall for people who claim to heal you, as you are to face all that comes your way and refine yourself through it. Healing happens when your consciousness shifts, though sometimes it does not happen because it is the karmic experience you are to go through. If you opt for rituals and other such solutions to your problems, you will disempower yourself more and will end up as someone else's energy source. Be aware, and may Siddha Blessings lead you to clarity and to natural solutions that you realise within.

Q: What do you think about Guru Siyag? He never asked money for his work. What is your opinion about mantra?

A: Whatever the marketing strategy, whether it is a free service or one based upon donation, everyone eats and requires some resources for their sustenance. The trick of offering a free service is to attract the masses. True knowledge is perverted by the unprepared and immature masses, and thus, it is only offered to more mature ones. This may appear to be an issue of superiority, but it is not. Many wise men refused to throw pearls before the swine, and that happened even just at the beginning of Kali Yuga. This is the age where truth cannot be recognised easily since there is no reference point for it. True masters are always taken care of by the nature of their free natural flow of expression.

Personally, I neither think of anything nor do I want to comment on anything as everything is always right. Everyone has their own level of refinement and perception and they see things from that limited perspective. Evolution continues, but it is important to remember the age that we are currently in.

Q: I like your enthusiasm for awakening and enlightenment, but please travel on the path completely before taking on the role of a teacher.

A: The mirror only reflects. A cat will never become a dog, and a cow will never be a human. In order to see beyond, we must work with reflections and challenges. Judgement comes to us first and is easier than Being. Try to be and you will see that all is already correct. The more you read that which does not make sense to your logical mind, the more there will be a chance that it will make sense to your Being, since logic, rigidity and conditionings of the mind obstruct the Being.

The world is not against 'I' when 'I' is not against the world. The truth hurts but also disillusions only that 'I' which is victimised and lives in separation and division from all. Look for Being and contentment rather than for division and opposition. True preceptors are rare and can only be recognised by the vibration and knowledge that flows out of their Being. All the rest just talk and spread delusion to those who expect and demand such delusion. In order to recognise all this, one needs to come empty-handed.

Q: How does Kundalini and Sada/Siva function through a spiritual master?

A: Kundalini Sada/Siva consciousness is for everyone. There is no space-time barrier in the quantum world. The Consciousness can take any name and form, but it always manifests in the same way, spontaneously and blissfully, anywhere, and especially through those who have tasted it and melted into it. When your individual consciousness concentrates on the form in which kundalini is active, you receive the current instantly. This is what makes this teaching still alive, as it has been passed on up until now from one activated being to others.

Q: How does a guru teach a disciple? Is it only through resonance and transmission?

A: It is the presence of the master and the readiness of the disciple that causes resonance. The guru *is* the presence of the master; it teaches through the master. Guru is for everyone; it is kundalini consciousness. Because it is Supreme, it addresses everyone in the way that they need, and this is why there are various teachings and perceptions. The essence remains untouched however, as it is pure and eternal. If you tune into the Essence you will find that the Essence is beyond knowledge and beyond perception, that it neither is nor is not.

Q: Practicing introspection and not deluding myself has changed me in the most profound way. The outcomes have all been very confusing, as I have no teacher; life is my teacher.

A: Life is always a teacher, even when you have an external teacher. Consciousness manifests distortions through your life circumstances, so you need to notice them and to transform them. Each layer that you notice means that it has come to the surface to be transformed. We are all collected here to experience the emotional reality and to refine it from within the self. Now is the time.

Q: Why do you teach? What philosophical ideas that already exist do not cover your ideas? The act of teaching is itself the last act of the ego that one has to be let go of.

A: I do not teach since there is nothing to teach. I am – so the sharing of the Being is just this. Some see it as teaching, and some choose to see it or interpret it through one prism or another. Yet, Being cannot be boxed; it can only be experienced. All that we see and learn is through our conditionings. By seeing this, and by recognising the limitations, we understand the unlimited. Without refining conditionings, one is not able to simply be. If you consider this to be teaching, then let it be so, but it is really a very simple universal truth that is as old as time. True spirituality is about Being; it is action-less in its essence, therefore hard to grasp. It is as simple, and as familiar and close to you as the breath passing through your nose.

REALISATION IN THE WORLD:
BECOMING THE NATURAL FLOW

Q: Why is the spiritual path so complicated in that you have to constantly evolve from one level to the next and may get stuck at one level for the rest of your life? The Siddha path, to me, seems very demanding and actually not simple at all.

A: We do not need to perceive the path as a linear one. Spiritual awakening is about awakening to our Natural Being and natural mind, which is absorbed into the Self, unconditional and beyond judgement. It is our Natural Being and not something that is to be forced. Being in contact with someone who maintains this being, not in a temporary way but in a way that they are established in it through their being, makes others able to perceive this too. No one is special; no one is inferior or superior, but some people are able to let go of logic and imagination and transcend, while others get stuck on the idea of concepts or bookish knowledge, drugs, or an overstimulated imagination – so they miss their natural, simple Being.

Q: I have had a snake phobia all my life. I've never been bitten or even been close to a snake before, but for some reason they are my biggest fear. Why do I have this phobia?

A: You must have had some past life experience that has been marked in your consciousness coming from a warning about or regarding the danger of snakes. It could also be something

175

ancestral. Accept the worst-case scenario and observe your feelings within regarding this phobia. Most snakes would never attack unless they feel they are in danger or the fear coming from others.

Cultivate inner peace towards any potential situation in your life. For example, when we are on an airplane, what can we do? We are fully at the mercy of the pilot. We have to learn to accept the flow of life as our best way to refine the self, as there is no difference between life and you. You contain everything within yourself because consciousness holds everything within.

Q: I need the support of a belief to make my thought stronger.

A: Why do you keep on disempowering yourself? All you need to understand is your own value, and to discipline your life. Tune into simplicity and stop scattering your attention outwards towards New Age nonsense and other ideas.

Life is simpler than you think. Look at Nature and learn from it – such simplicity, and such sophistication at the same time! The Natural World is the best support and the way to navigate in life. This Natural World is not only what you see or observe; it is what you perceive beyond the sensory observation – harmony and balance. The reality of true human existence is free from thoughts and emotional imbalances; it is equanimous, content, intelligent being. Stop supporting your current imbalances by generating the same thoughts on and on, and by invoking the same emotions on and on. Stop and be in stillness, observe nature, and accept the simplicity of life. Then, clarity will prevail.

Q: My cat has kidney failure and needs urgent healing, will you please help?

A: I can only help with healing the attachment. Life shows us things that trigger our imperfections, while at the same time pointing the way to perfection. Animals know how to heal themselves, and if they cannot, then they simply withdraw. Do not project your human perception onto animals, but just wish the cat well and trust the natural flow of life. Nature has immense power to take care of itself.

Q: I am currently in a perpetual loop of integration and disintegration. How do I refine and stabilise?

A: When one becomes aware of the equanimous Self-Being, one is able to see the veils of the self. This process is called refinement. One goes back and forth from stillness to emotional heights and back to stillness; in this way one learns to understand the transitory nature of all phenomena and learns to recognise the permanent Being of the self. This process is called sadhana – spiritual practice. One cultivates patience and the acceptance of life for what it is, seeing every moment as a new opportunity to learn, experience, understand and refine the transitory perception of the self. Is this not exciting? If one is able to consciously do this, then one becomes a diligent student of life and is eventually able to break through all the self-created illusions.

Q: Pain and pleasure should neither be avoided nor pursued. The truth is the middle way. The desire for pleasure and pain are the driving forces in our lives. The beginning of self-realisation lies in the desire to find freedom after the experience of not being free in pain and suffering. This can be brought about through the practice of self-observation and contemplation. The more you are in the resulting altered states, the more you can recreate them at any time, and the more these states will influence others. Most people are afraid of such states. That is why it is tricky to deal with most people, unless they are prepared to experience these different states of mind.

A: Desire and pain are relative; they are as they are, and only seem to exist simply because we interpret them as such. They are ever-changing concepts, and what one considers as desire, the other pursues as attachment. What one sees as suffering, the other thinks of as pleasure. An attachment to anything brings bondage. Attachment operates through such feelings as guilt, shame and longing. Fear and anger are even worse. All of these feelings come from attachment. Suffering helps us to get rid of attachment, and it is the driving force in our spiritual evolution and should not be avoided. It should be observed and accepted as a part of life and reconsidered because of this role it plays.

When consciousness shifts, everything changes, and life becomes about being content and watching the drama with detachment. This does not mean that one cannot enjoy it. It means that one can enjoy as well as suffer, and that one has no attachment to either, because one treats all as the equal outcomes of life. When this happens, the soul is ripened, where one's individual perception of the limited soul expands and goes beyond its limitations to awaken and grow.

Q: How can we know if we are making progress and breaking through obstacles? I feel that I have many blind spots when it comes to identifying the root causes of my life-issues. Is there anything I can do to improve and be more successful in my self-healing?

A: If we want to break through, then we need to surrender our judgement and our desire to act, into Being. Sometimes there is nothing much to do but to be. Through this Being, clarity and our true essence comes forth.

There is no need to compare ourselves to others, only to try to understand what it is that we are truly inclined towards, so that only then we may see what vision we may build upon it. Having a vision is important, but in order to have a clear vision we have to be balanced and absorbed into the self, so that we then truly know what is there within us that truly calls us to act.

The process of self-refinement is eternal, and it happens on various levels. In accepting the fact that our life is an evolutionary journey, we stop projecting something onto spirituality that it is not. When we vibrate purity, non-judgement and natural bliss, then healing and teaching become a natural way of being and of expressing self without any pomp or desire.

Q: What are the spiritual implications of having sexual intercourse?

A: Overall, it is healthy when the minds and bodies of both people are refined and in contentment. In general, it is important to use every organ consciously, and when it comes to the sexual organs, if the natural bodily release comes only once in a while, then it is fine. But who you are having sex with matters. If the person is afflicted in any way, you will exchange such energy or may connect with such an affliction. It is an exchange, but the question arises, an exchange of what? This exchange happens on various levels because you connect with a being who is linked to their ancestral lines and more. Remember that all problems arise from not having a clear direction and from not knowing what one wants.

Q: What are your views on some of the popular contemporary mystics?

A: When your perception is cleared, then you will definitely know who is who, and what such figures are all about. Having a view on something is a general idea about something or someone based on an external sense perception, and if this view has no subtlety or depth, then it is based on judgement. Judging is a waste of time and conscious energy. The more you cultivate stillness and dwell in your Natural Being, the more you will perceive the nature of this illusion that we call 'reality'. By doing this, you will come to know the 'agents' of this illusion.

People like to create names and tags for themselves, yet there is nothing behind these. The current illusion is well-planned and is pure psychological manipulation. Those who realise this, see everything as it is (and as it is not) conveyed by others or by the mainstream. As long as you are a part of the collective delusion, you have no mind of your own, even if you think you do.

Q: Do you have any siddhis?

A: I do not have any siddhis, nor am I any sort of special person. I am a student of life and existence and I express myself and share without any aim and in a spontaneous way as knowledge arises within.

You do not need to have siddhis to perceive Reality in an equanimous and unconditional way. Your mind simply needs to be pure and unconditional, aimless (in the logical-human or linear context) and selfless. When you are as selfless as existence, you are the existence and know everything effortlessly without a need or a desire to know.

Q: How do you define patience? What are the ways a person can practice it in the short and long term?

A: Patience is acceptance and understanding that everything is temporary. We can practice it sometimes by having compassion towards ignorant beings, sometimes by letting go of the emotional waves within. It depends on the situation. Why focus on patience, why not on letting go? Sometimes we need to draw the right boundaries with people or with our habits, so in these cases patience is not the solution.

Q: It seems that my entire family is here to challenge me very profoundly. The more I feel like an empty vessel that is free from judging, the more judgement seems to be all around me. How can I deal with this and remain calm? Am I on the right path?

A: The problem is that you have changed, and your more equanimous state reflects their victimisation. It is a test for you, to either fall for an old program when someone's thoughts and words make you feel bad, or to stay in your own contentment. The more we try to refine, the more other people will start seeing their own victimisation and negativity mirrored from you. The most important thing is to agree and leave. Do not act passive-aggressively as it also does no good.

People want to hustle and gossip, and if they do not have this or cannot get an emotional charge from you, then they will turn against you and gossip about you. Maybe the state you are in now requires you to live more independently. My advice is not to take it to heart. You should simply see that all they say to you is what they think of themselves. You reflect, with your equanimous empty state, their problems, and the reason they are angry is that they refuse to face themselves, and so your presence simply becomes of an irritating nature. They do not even realise it, but you should realise this yourself.

They want to emotionally engage with you and dump their negative feelings, and they get no response. Outwardly, they do not get you, but inwardly you still seem to feel hurt, and you react. Work on it and neutralise the responses more. You will understand that if you are sure about what you are and are content and do not doubt your inner being (and thus the path), then no other element from this world can doubt or challenge it either.

Q: I think that more than any feelings of energy, a change in the interpretation of one's perceptions is a better sign of spiritual evolution, is it not?

A: True spirituality is never about feeling energy or pursuing any type of feeling. It is about the experience of the natural, blissful Being, and about reconnecting with this Being and self-refining so that it culminates in simplicity, selflessness and self-mastery. Self-mastery leads to the perfection of the body and to the ability to consciously liberate oneself at the end of one's life from this trap-like existence.

Most people do not know what life or death is. Exiting the physical body is not death. Through inner transformation, one learns about life from within, and learns how to exit this illusory reality so that one further continues one's evolution as an evolved spiritual being. Wasting time on pursuing concepts, powers, and techniques does not lead one to any evolution or realisation, only to further entanglement with the experience. Learn to dwell in stillness and the simple, blissful equanimity of the self, and you will know everything without the desire to know.

Q: Are we ever fully safe in this world?

A: You are safe to the degree of your inner purity, selflessness and trust in the Higher Being.

Q: I got into an intellectual discussion recently that turned into a prolonged argument. I felt foolish afterwards for playing this role. How can I avoid these situations?

A: When it comes to arguments, try to follow them back to the root. The root is the desire to be right, to be acknowledged and to be seen as knowledgeable. The most important thing is that all of these are the past. No one knows things exactly; evidence changes, people assume and speculate depending on their intellectual, spiritual and emotional levels. Thus, there is no such thing as being right. Everyone has an opinion and a viewpoint, but since they are based on the past, it might be irrelevant for the actual present and thus futile and energy-draining.

Try to let go of such waves within whenever they arise. No experience is ever lost, nor is it good or bad. Every moment just brings us a new perspective, especially if we are aware of it. So, cultivate stillness and learn to step out of each moment and be aware of the present only. Then, absorption and contentment will always be there.

Q: Every time I see an animal suffering, I am filled with sadness, but I now understand that I have to own that pain and dissolve it in the light of silence. But still, my mind thinks of this as a subtle escape from the pain and from helping the animals. How does this 'bringing of suffering back to ourselves' help the world?

A: You have understood that even positive emotions are of an illusory nature, as both good and bad emotions entrap. Stillness, equanimity and contemplating on the transitory nature of all phenomena will make you understand that compassion and the desire to help others against their will, along with interfering in any way in the lives of others that is not based on wisdom and that is not detached in a healthy way, only leads to entanglements, suffering and to more bondage.

Wise people know that 'everything is always right.' Deal with the waves that arise in the space of your own self only. If you are asked for this help and can render this help, then help selflessly and forget. Uproot victimisation patterns, false ideas and projections, and then you will plunge into the deep stillness of the blissful and empty contented Being.

184

Q: Do souls have a gender? Could the soul's gender be the cause for issues like gender dysphoria?

A: All this is speculation. In order to understand what is what, one needs to go beyond the pre-conceived ideas and the man-made reality and various speculations, and into the Ultimate Reality through turning one's own consciousness within: absorption. Through contemplation in absorbed Being, all the answers about the self and the creation arise spontaneously with time. This is called self-born knowledge, the knowledge which is a conscious emanation within and that does not come from any logical assumptions, stories or agendas of others. Cultivate inner stillness and refine self. Then everything will get clearer and clearer.

Q: I know some people who go to yoga classes almost every day; they have spent many thousands towards their progress and still nothing has happened. Their life is the same, nothing has changed, and there has been no inner shift.

A: A paradox indeed. The whole of life is a paradox. The more you chase something, the more it runs away from you. Once you stop – you understand that it has been there at all times – so it is with the true Being and with natural spirituality. The more ambition – the less realisation.

Q: I am ashamed of the actions of my past and the ignorance and selfishness which has led me to bad decisions and to the mistreatment of people who only wanted the best for me. I beat myself up every day because I live in regret. I still feel incomplete and disconnected from God.

185

A: Firstly, understand that you are taken care of, that you have survived until now, and that you will survive in the future. God is all that which is manifested, and that which is beyond the manifestation. All those experiences, situations, dramas and people you feel guilt, shame and regret towards are part of the manifestation. It is just an experience that you had to go through to get here. You need to learn to step over it and let go. Learn to wish your past well and to move forward. There is nothing that we can do, and nothing needs to be done. Everyone involved in your past had a choice and acted and made decisions in the way that they could at that moment. Whatever has happened should be let go, or else you will attract and revive this past on and on, and this will result in the draining of the subtle body and the corruption of the physical. Through the condemnation of people, you will enable those souls who have left you to disturb you. Let the situation go; learn to forgive the self and others and move on. Learning from this means that you no longer do such things, that you realise what pushed you to do it in the first place and thus, you understand your distortions.

You are a pure Being that has become corrupt. The Pure Being is there at all times, and by cultivating inner stillness you are able to come back to it and resolve all the issues within. By understanding this, you allow the self to evolve further. Everything that matters exists only in the present moment, so stop dragging the past behind you as if it were an iron ball and chain. Let go. From a higher perspective, nothing happened, and all this human drama has no meaning.

Q: What is your view on Eckhart Tolle?

A: There is no view. The less refined we are, the more views we have on things. The more refined we are, the clearer we can perceive, and the less we can be deluded. Wise people look into and cultivate only their own gardens. True spirituality is free from ambitions and comparisons, greed, envy, or imposition. It is selfless and natural like the flow of life itself.

There is true spirituality and there is false spirituality. True spirituality is born in silence and absorption and is only known within. Through this comes the basis for clarity, where one sees everything as it is in a true light and as an extension of the self.

False spirituality fosters having points of view and taking sides. It wants to please and to appease various groups by having opinions that are either super-positive or super-negative, which end up deluding one more. Abstain from opinions and extremes and cultivate stillness and pure perception. Then you will know. Once you know, why would you talk about such things? Let delusion play its role and let existence exist.

Q: Does purification only occur with the help of contemplation/meditation? Does it mean that we do not have to do any physical exercises like running or other activities?

A: True refinement happens only through absorption into blissful emptiness – samadhi. Samadhi is not an achievement; it is our Natural Being through which we refine. If you wish to run, exercise, stretch, or do anything voluntary, that is up to you. Only deep absorption and refinement will lead to transformation, immortality and the possibility of liberation. Whatever you feel is right in a particular moment, you can consciously do or not do. Doing is a part of life. Doing through awareness and stillness leads one to making no errors.

Q: How can I heal if I have a friend who has negative energy and I have been affected by him? I started having pain in my cervical area, headaches, and cravings. How can I help my friend, or how can I rebalance myself with energy?

A: Heal and balance yourself first. Refine yourself in order to know who is who and what is what. If one is not able to see the roots of one's own issues, then how can one see the roots of suffering in others? It will be a case of the blind leading the blind. Let people have their own experience and understanding. Siddhas never heal or interfere with other beings' lives. They perceive the multidimensional reality of each and every being and know all the so-called suffering and other phenomena that is created and propelled by these beings. Life is about freewill, and everyone lives this freewill and the choices they make to the fullest.

Why would you want to interfere or help? Question your motives – is it control? Do you want to change anyone? It is futile to do this, as people have their own experience to go through and no one should interfere with it. Even Almighty Creation, with all its power, stands still and does not interfere, so why would you?

Maturity naturally arises through one's natural evolution in life, and by seeing all of one's personal distortions – whether seen as suffering or as joy – in the course of one's life. Before the time is right for them, a person will not be able to understand the essence of this, and so they will be driven by unrefined emotions – empathy entrapped in fears, the need to control, and a corrupt sense of self-victimisation.

Trying to change the world without refining one's own perception leads one to self-deception, ego, delusion, and to a dead-end. Turn within and cultivate inner stillness. Then, you will understand the roots of your own suffering and the suffering of the other. With time, you may grow to the point of understanding that there is no suffering or joy; there is only a natural projection of all the conscious distortions that people interpret as suffering or happiness. Everything is always right and balanced in its core.

Q: I have been experiencing very small kriyas lately as I have been deepening in my practice. I have been finding that my practice is becoming integrated into my life more and more every day. Is this what is referred to as sadhana becoming sadhana?

A: True spirituality is Natural Being, so it should not contradict our normal life. The problems happen when our life is not happening within the natural flow or cycles and is not organic. In natural circumstances, we would not need to practice anything, nor worship nor project our power elsewhere, but due to the fact that we are degraded, spirituality has become a form and process of restoration back towards the Natural Being. So, when life is like this, we are just awakening to the Natural Being and trying to integrate it within our lives as much as possible. The further into the process of refinement one is, the more one simplifies and disillusions, and thus realises what this reality and illusion are. Yet, there is a need for a breakthrough at some point, and this is where grace and deeper readiness are needed.

Everything happens at the right time. You are on a path of self-exploration and refinement. The more you let go of false projections and illusions, the more you will see how simple and absolutely intelligent everything is.

Q: Thank you for your help! Blessings to you for releasing us from ourselves and from the illusions of what others do to us.

A: Blessings. No one can truly free or release us, unless we perceive the Ultimate within our being and through it, understand the illusions, delusions and madness of the current human existence. Make choices every day and be responsible for your life since there are no saviours and no solutions outside of the self. One may be reminded or guided to such a realisation from the outside, but the actual direct experience and realisation of what is what only comes from within. The best way is to learn to take responsibility for everything you experience in life and to gradually abandon victimised programs and patterns of behaviour that lead to emotional and mental entanglements with the reality which is purely neutral in its essence.

Q: You say that men and women need to cultivate different virtues in order to go beyond gender. As a male, when I look at myself, I get the impression that I have a lot of the qualities of both genders and do not feel that gentleness is what is missing. Is it really that simple that the physical body is the decisive aspect?

A: If the body and the limited mind were not the decisive aspects, then who would bother to struggle for 'enlightenment' and try to expand and to break through limitations? Spirituality is in many ways a transformative bio-chemical process. In order to understand this, we need to go beyond gender awareness. But before we do this, we need to be perfectly aware as to what the body and our gender are for. We also need to know how to unleash the potential that our bodies carry by being in a purified state of awareness.

We are born in a physical body which is subjected to gender, and this body is the manifestation of the limited mind and its impressions, distortions and so on. When we do spiritual practice, we work with these distortions and impressions, and without having a deep understanding of them, we cannot go into equanimity and blissful awareness. While in blissful awareness, you can be aware of your body but not be influenced by the negative currents it may generate, unless there is a need for the body to be used as a tool or for service to others, and so forth.

Q: Does the body give you the real clue as to the mind's limitations? I feel that the gender polarity that you speak of does not apply to everyone since there can be very strong women and very gentle men. Is this correct?

A: Every man has to clearly see his level of strength and aggressiveness and become gentler if that is needed. If a man is gentler, then they have more of a chance to cultivate spiritual wisdom as, often, such men can go naturally beyond their gender and their aggressive and animalistic natures. And it is the same with very sensitive and emotional (especially negatively emotional) women. They need to observe their emotions more carefully and work with their sensitivities in order to understand what the karmic roots of these emotions are. Then they can eventually go beyond them through cultivating inner strength and what are commonly thought of as more masculine qualities. This will result in neutrality and an inner spiritual strength which is beyond gender. When we lack something, we need to add whatever is missing so that we become balanced.

Q: Do things like fun and novelty still occur for someone who has achieved a state of equanimity and integrated blissful contentment, or do those sorts of things fall aside and lose importance?

A: Life is constantly fun in its natural form. There is nothing that needs to be added to it or subtracted from it. If we cannot see this fun in everything we do, then we are not content within. If we are not content within, then we will try to find an explanation and try to fill in our lives with everything possible, from food to stimulants, movies, art, entertaining spirituality, drugs, etc.

Life is beautiful in each moment, and even during the challenging moments if you are aware of the self. You may look at everything as fun if you wish. After all, you give everything meaning. Work on the perception, as it defines everything you experience. You may do anything you want as long as you are content, aware and fully responsible for all you do and experience, and as long as you are able to let it all go in the next moment. All our desires and inclinations are the past that we have to refine. If you realise this, then you will let these things go and see the novelty in each moment and each breath of your being.

Q: Do you think that masturbating will impede my path? I hear conflicting ideas on this, with some saying that it will impede the life-force and others saying that it is great for overall bio-spiritual health.

A: Masturbation is a natural way to release excessive energy, but the imagination and stories that impel one to masturbate need to be understood. You need to see what pushes you to do it if it is done more than is necessary and in an obsessive manner. Certain internal feelings such as victimisation and anger may be at its root. But natural release, without any reasons and without any imagination being involved, is a way to balance one's energies, as is having healthy sexual interaction with a healthy and balanced human being. The problem is that it is rare nowadays to find a healthy human being who is balanced on all levels and free from afflictions. If one is not free from afflictions, through having sex together, people can exchange these afflictions or get entangled on subtler levels.

Love is contentment, so sex should sprout out from having a true spiritual and intellectual connection and through deep internal contentment and not from being lustful. Then, such physical experience will be health-promoting and nourishing rather than being an act of entanglement and further drama. The true loss of power happens through projecting mentally, through the outward-dispersion of conscious power, and by clinging.

The true essence of sexual interaction cannot be grasped unless one is refined, equanimous and evolved. When one is like this, then sex will not be seen in the same way as the majority of people view it nowadays, nor will it be exploited in any way. Sex is a true science of creation and procreation, but when people approach it with lustful instincts, victimisation, or perversion, then they cannot understand its essence, and they see it as addictive. True sexuality is self-expression to the degree that one understands the self. If one understands and is aware of the self only on the gross-emotional level, then that is a limited understanding.

Q: Do you ever smile and have fun? I get the feeling that I have to be scared thinking about or talking to others when I listen to your videos.

A: I definitely have fun, as life, as a flow, comes from being a content and blissful Being. When you are absorbed into this, you will understand. Scratching on the surface and looking for external positivity leads you to misconceptions about life. Life is not about positive or negative, having fun or not having fun. Life itself is a beautiful emanation which does not need to be boxed into categories of good or bad. Such a notion comes from having an obscured human perception and perspective on reality. Absorption into the Ultimate Being awakens one to the flow of life beyond such notions. The expression and facial form of an absorbed blissful being does not always conform to the expectations of those who dwell on emotions and who have limited judgement.

Life is truly a joy when one lives to the fullest, but one can only do so when one has realised and known the essence of Reality rather than just dwelling in a man-made emotional illusion. True emotions are there at all times because they are part of the embodied consciousness, but for most, they become deluding and enslaving forces, as they are impure and are expressed through personal stories.

When you perceive something, you should be sceptical about knowing that thing, because if you perceive without creating stories and without the desire to see what you want to see, then you will perceive the truth. Our projected reality is not static, so go beyond the projection and you will understand.

Q: Who knows how long we will live, we could all drop dead tomorrow.

A: Life and death are subjected to our obscured perspective on existence. Awareness exists throughout all perspectives, states of mind and various life experiences. One should contemplate on this and try to concentrate on being rather than on the division of existence into life or death. People neither know how to live nor how to die. Death is not understood for what it is due to the ignorance of our existence.

Q: Is celibacy required to become enlightened?

A: If you are Consciousness, you are everything and nothing at the same time. As you have the body overall, which requires things to sustain itself, so you have the stomach, the sexual organs, and other organs that support proper and harmonious body function. True celibacy is the way you maintain the power of consciousness; it is about whether you contain it or project it. If you know the science of consciousness – the light-matter of the self – then you know the science of stillness, equanimity and the gradual enlightening of the entire body.

Sexual celibacy is misunderstood by the current populations who are engrossed in ignorance and lust. True sexuality is an expression of the self on all levels – emotional, bodily, mental, intellectual, spiritual; and the part of it that is the sexual act is only a very small part of it. The real problem regarding celibacy lies in the distorted, outward-going consciousness that wastes energy on resolving the illusory phenomena of the self.

Q: How did this crazy thing called life occur in the first place? Also, I find myself sleeping a lot after reading your book.

A: This world is the result of the currently corrupt collective consciousness. Turbulent waves within the self cause turbulence in the outside world, and the people and circumstances that manifest in one's life are just triggers and external catalysts that show us this turbulence. Try to find inner contentment through trying not to judge, through trying not to change the world or others. Let go of control and the desire to interfere and to demonstrate, to become anyone or anything. Then, life will appear simpler and easier to deal with.

Conquer laziness and procrastination by acting through the contented Being. Sleeping occurs due to the fact that your consciousness is unable to remain aware during the deeper absorption into Being, so that when this absorption happens, you plunge into sleep. Try to walk more and to drink good quality water; eat healthy as well and have no stimulants so that, with time, you will be able to withstand the strong vibrations that come from the book.

Q: I have noticed that always having access to everything almost devalues information; when I find information on all kinds of yoga for free online, it makes such things less special so that they lose their magic.

A: Whenever we recognise the value of something, the thought of not being able to afford it falls away automatically. Everything happens at the right time. Due to the power of the self, grace, and the intent to evolve, we eventually come across genuine information. Information does not transform; it may expand awareness or give various perspectives on a subject, but in order to be able to discriminate as to what is what, we have to awaken to the truth within and decipher what is true and what is false, to contemplate on ourselves and to refine the self through self-observation.

Q: Is it good to serve others? What is selfless service?

A: Service is service, as any act is neutral in itself, yet people give it the colour of good or bad, useful or useless, right or wrong. When such assumptions as these are not there, then service is just service and is therefore selfless. You should have a vision, do what you like, and then forget about what you have done. This is the way to selflessly express the self in this world. Words are always limited, therefore transmissions are the best way to learn for those who can perceive such a thing.

Q: What is your view on life after the physical death, and what does one's experience then become?

A: Why are you thinking about what happens after this life when life is always happening now in each breath? If you have thoughts of an afterlife, then those thoughts are what you are going to be living at some point in time and space. All is imaginary.

In order to grasp the essence of life, stay in the present, stay in your body and be relaxed and feel within, then you will see the truth. In order to understand the manifestation of the self, you need to know the process that makes it happen. Even though you may grasp such a thing intellectually, it will merely be information to you without inner awakening and the realisation of who you are throughout your daily experience. It does not matter what you do or what you think or believe in, because such things are not really you but are only your artificially-created identities. When you free yourself from these identities, you perceive the self in an unobstructed way, as a flow of consciousness that is always neutral, neither over-excited nor depressed.

Q: I have gone through the process of following spiritual knowledge from books and other sources and it has been very, very difficult to understand. I have accumulated so much garbage in my mind and have been repeating things that I read like a parrot. I have performed constant sadhana over the years and had transmissions of shaktipat, but everything has been garbage and not useful to me. I am now experiencing the state of absorption so that I do not need to create and search for concepts, and have found immense treasures inside myself which are not like anything I have read. In my circle of family and friends, there is a lot of pain and suffering, and I wonder why I cannot express such great experiences to them in order to help them. Is spirituality selfish? Should the people around me live their own lives and discover their own process?

A: Everyone walks their own path, but if they look for help, ask for it and are genuine about it, then you may help them. Such help is to be based on non-violence, where one is to remain selfless and compassionately detached from those who one helps, without creating any emotional ties. True help is non-emotional; it is refined and truly spiritual, and it does not demonstrate itself. It appears on its own, sometimes as a miracle, without announcing itself. Your absorption and higher meditative states will naturally transform your surroundings, provided that your surroundings are receptive to and enjoy your Being. These high vibrations can create a miracle without your 'I' necessarily being actively involved.

Q: Can we use prayer in order to help us attain qualities that will make us more self-aware, qualities such as courage, understanding, clarity and wisdom?

A: A common human problem is the inability to accept our life experience as it is. Hence, we pray; we want to control and manoeuvre life in the direction that we think is the correct one. But our thoughts are conditioned by ideas, concepts and dogmas that come from society, religion and our family, so we do not really know anything.

Only through inner awakening are we gradually able to come out of these conditionings and limitations, and accept whatever experience comes our way and embrace it for what it is. In that moment, we obtain great understanding about the world, the self, and the manifestation. This is very difficult to achieve for the great majority of people on Earth, but it is the reason we are here.

Q: It is very hard for me to understand what is going on within. I am always analysing what is happening, and because of this, I am sleep-deprived. I also feel odd sensations in my body as if there is an alien living within me which can be quite disturbing.

A: When one's lifestyle is imbalanced, the body suffers, fatigue accumulates, and it is hard to comprehend reality in a proper way. From that point, everything may seem depressive and gloomy. However, you must use your willpower and bring balance to your routine. Make an effort to have discipline in your life and in your approach to everyday chores. Respect your body and give it proper nourishment and sleep.

Q: Relaxation is the most difficult thing. I try to relax and wait every day for the moment when it arrives. I run and walk for hours just so as to be able to relax.

A: When there is restlessness, one is not able to perceive one's essence. Spiritual awakening results in inner stillness and a profound blissful contentment from which one's journey begins. But this journey is full of traps, so one needs to dedicate one's consciousness to self-observation and refinement, both through spiritual activities like observation and contemplation, as well as through being in absorption. At some point, one reaches the integration of doing through Being. Then, one is relaxed at all times, and is also able to perform tasks and chores, and to remain humble and selfless.

Q: I wanted to help a family member who is deeply entangled and influenced, but most of the time it is hard to even help myself. I understand that I have to take full responsibility, but it is easier said than done. I am thankful for having access to so much wisdom instead of just falling into a downward spiral of victimisation like I did in the past.

A: You will be fine once you realise that every emotion, issue, addiction and pain is a step towards your liberation, provided that you are aware and responsible for all the actions and reactions you have. When someone leaves us, we have to respect their freewill, but have they really left you if they are still within your space of awareness? No – because you are still tangled with them.

Let go and learn to be autonomous. Understand your childhood insecurities and come out of them. Stop longing, as you are actually longing for your own Being. Only in contentment can we be happy in our relationships with others. You can never lose anything within the space of the self because everything is reinforced by your own mind within itself. Your own mind entangles you with everything, whether people are physically there or are gone. You have neither let your self be free, nor have you let them live freely. Let them go and be happy about their choices, as this is the only way out and the way to the cure.

Q: Can we make our creative and our spiritual goals one?

A: It depends on the level of your spiritual intelligence and the understanding of how your intelligence can be integrated into your existence on the grosser levels. In essence, creativity and spirituality are the same; they represent a grosser and a subtler form of the same Consciousness. You can be spiritually creative or creatively spiritual – the first can be applied to adepts, the latter to artists.

Q: I strive to experience even a thousandth of your accomplishment in this life.

A: By the grace and the sincerity that are beyond the conditions and traps of this world, you might. Start cultivating purity and selflessness, which means no conditions and no thought of wanting to be anything. Just learn to see value in what you already have. Do not think that by scratching around the surface and by collecting information, even if it seems to be of a spiritual nature, you will evolve. True evolution is so subtle and is not anything to be proud of. If you want to be a king, a clown or a doctor of illusion, go ahead, but it has nothing to do with true spirituality.

Learn to simply be. You do not need other people's accomplishments, so why look into their gardens? Cultivate your own garden and learn through life and through your own body, while every day being present and aware, conscious and selfless. How do you wish to grasp the unconditional selfless purity of Siddha Being if that is not within yourself? Let go of all the rubbish you have accumulated and perceive the wholesomeness of Being. This will be the first step. Sit now and perceive.

Q: Thank you. Honestly, listening and reading to what you say sparks a joy in me every single day. The essence of your words makes me feel full. I really love that. If there is anything I can say to you that I know to be true, it is that. If I did not listen to your words, I would probably be depressed deep inside. I hope I will be worthy of whatever it is that you say in your videos and words one day. Well, thank you. And yes, I will do my best.

A: Look for the wholesomeness (completeness) within and realise your essence. All that which you see so far as outside of the self, is within the Self. Thus, look for it unconditionally, without expectations and ambitions, and you will discover it naturally and most unexpectedly.

Q: Through my own delusion, distortions, biased understanding, you have always represented something different, something that is too unusual and powerful to be described. You are a source of inspiration, strength, creativity — a true reminder of the importance of self-honesty to my ego-driven self. You have been a challenge and yet a true, authentic and loving guide, even if I have never met you. I am eternally grateful Jivanmukti, thank you for your passion, for your presence, for your guidance, for your service, freely given to those who dwell in ignorance. Thank you.

A: Deep recognition within you of the very fact that there is something to work on within is a big step forward towards a deeper awakening and self-refinement. Yet, in fact, any moment may become that very point of shift and dissolution of a pattern or layer of the inner illusion. Nothing is static, and our pure essence is always there at all times as the Ultimate Reality, even if at this very moment it seems inaccessible or veiled (usually due to turbulent emotions, conceptual knowledge, ambitions of the mind, etc.).

The more we accept life as it is, remain flexible, free from rigidity, dedicated to letting go, open and consciously flowing through every experience, the more we realise the essence of the pathless path within, and the more we feel responsible and cherish each moment of existence in the body. Honesty to the self is what makes one a true adept of life. Many blessings to you and best wishes on your path.

EPILOGUE

Q: Namaste. I hope you are doing well, and I thank you for sharing your deep views, knowledge and experiences as well as for your good wishes. I find your transmissions very interesting, helpful and mostly true. A few statements created questions and thoughts that I have posted below. I would find it interesting and pleasing should you choose to read and comment on them.

If I comprehend you correctly, you are saying that being victimised, hurt, alone etc., is the outcome of the individual's subconscious and conscious conception of life and choice? If so, were the colonised, the enslaved, the raped and murdered, and the ones suffering from hunger and sickness actually experiencing such things because they chose and/or believed that they must experience such things? Are dictators, murderers, paedophile rapists and abusive parents etc., then doing the 'right thing' because that is what the 'victims' ask for? Are the victims creating their perpetrators?

A: The answer is yes. This is the day and age when everyone experiences what they are supposed to experience due to past entanglements. This requires a deeper understanding of what reality is, beyond the physical notions of reality and its human interpretation.

How do you know that the one who is raped or abused today has not done it themselves at an earlier time? There is only one truth, and that is that everything is right at every point in time. We live through the experience, and every experience becomes individually interpreted, yet it does not mean that that is exactly what is happening. Social events and experiences are conveyed through history books, but their happening as we are told is not necessarily the truth. Because people are very limited and ignorant in this day and age; through their having no access to or understanding of the subtler realms of existence, they cannot truly understand what is going on, and they perceive and interpret everything through a very limited human perspective based on imbalanced emotions and supported by limited thought patterns that are themselves based on limited concepts, socially accepted modalities of existence, beliefs, cultural backgrounds, etc.

After all, those who write the history are those who are the victors. Those who win portray themselves as good-hearted and caring and wipe out the truth of everything else. Thus, history is incomplete. Those who cannot access the subtler realms will never know the subtle reasons behind every action and every phenomenon existing in the physical reality.

Q: Does it all mean that the so-called 'victims' are the actual perpetrators, and that these 'victims' actually want trauma, despotism, and judgment to come upon them because they are suicidal and extremely mentally sick? Are their 'perpetrators' then their self-made 'heroes/demons' coming to grant them their wishes or to relieve them of their agony? What a crazy thought! Consequently, is true contentment within God, Gods teachings, and living in faith that God will create paradise on Earth? Wouldn't this also bind us on the earthly plane?

A: This life experience only invokes the trauma that exists and has existed before this birth. By invoking this trauma, one has a chance to resolve it and to dissolve it within the self; if not, one dives even deeper into a victimised state. This day and age is one of corruption, and thus, everyone can live and relive their corruption on and on. Why? Because in this way, one gets a new chance to understand the corruption and the inner mechanism that supports it from within. Everyone who faces various experiences could simply let go of them and move on, yet doing this is not simple and requires a crucial change in our social system and our level of accepting certain things in society that pass as being either normal or an anomaly.

Personally, I think this current society represents an organised social madness where more and more perversion (that which is instigated and propelled through dysfunctional families, suppressed religious thinking, drugs, and the modern age of imbalanced sexuality) is accepted for normality. Our education system does not look in this direction, and so the outcome is what it is. Since this is so, what do you expect when being born here?

Even now, through reading this, through being in a victimised mode of perception, one is not ready to see the truth but instead has an inner wave that defends their own point of view, ideas and beliefs. Such an attitude holds in its core, the preconceived idea and righteousness that blinds one and does not allow one to see everything in an expanded and more unconditional and neutral way. One accepts and wants to hear only that which they are ready to hear whilst denying everything else, or one starts fighting and generating more negativity without realising it, thus creating more conflict from which one may become the victim.

The inability to neutrally perceive the reality and be able to let go of any experience, makes current people limited and deeply imbalanced. They create a story and roam in these past stories on and on, forgetting to live. What is life? Life is every new moment at every moment of existence. And yet, what the majority does is drag each moment behind them so that it becomes a heavy ball and chain over time that drains them, ages them, and pushes them towards self-destructive and self-punishing ways of living.

Q: Why even care about health when life is supposedly about preparing to leave forever and overcome whatever is holding you on the earthly plane? Why even care about anyone or anything when this only keeps you on the earthly plane? Why be given a mind, body, heart and soul if it is, supposedly, all about becoming nothingness and merely existing like a hollow shell? Is a hollow shell filled with information or life? Is a hollow nothingness capable of feeling, giving or receiving any compassion or love? Could nothingness lead to contentment? How can nothingness create life and bring forth children? Are you content? Are you lonely in nothingness? Does nothingness fulfil your Soul?

A: Eternal Being is a blissful, equanimous and absolutely content Being, but emotionally imbalanced people are dormant to such existence. Your question is born from this limited perspective and perception. As long as you nurture such views and do not allow yourself to simply be for a moment in stillness, you keep on exhausting yourself and loading yourself with all sorts of information that is convenient for you and that feeds your victimised being. Through such an approach, there is no healing or refinement but more and more entanglement, ever-growing imbalance, and thus disease, inflammation and decay. You could instead, let go of all that fight, and bathe in natural, pure blissful Being and evolve in spiritual intelligence. All depends on where your focus is and what your priorities are.

When one evolves, one evolves out of the limited human perception of reality that divides this reality into good and bad, holy and evil and that propels further conflict. The actual reality is neutral, and nothingness is the wholesome Being that is deeply content, intelligent and aware, and is immortal existence itself. We are inseparable from this existence. The only thing that separates us from it is our preoccupation with the world that we corrupt and propel from within because we do not like or agree with it. Where is this all coming from if not from the collectivised corrupt self?

There is no you and 'your soul', and there is no nothingness. You divide reality and thus see it in fragments. Nothingness is called so because it does not have any connection within your individual being so far (with the illusory reality), and yet it is the most fulfilling and wholesome immortal existence, the existence which also brings longevity to the physical. What keeps you on the earthly plane is your ignorance and emotions. Everyone understands this from their own evolutionary standpoint and limitations, and thus, their life is lived accordingly.

Whatever the motive may be, it keeps one here, including even the best motives. True evolution starts when we do not have a motive but start awakening to the illusion of our existence and see the falsehood. We eventually understand that all this falsehood comes from within – or at least is supported from within – and contributes to the collective. When one understands this, one shifts one's priorities from the external projected world to the actual real world within, and understands that even this real world within is veiled and polluted and needs refinement in order for its true essence (which is NOTHING from the point of view of the corrupt world) to shine through and restore the perception of wholesomeness within the individual self/existence.

Health or true wellbeing is the result of one's spiritual refinement, where one's subtle being, which is engrossed in karmic impressions is refined, and where the result of this refinement is a rejuvenated and youthful being. The physical aspect of health is impossible without the refinement of the subtle being or the letting go or dissolving of internal subtle distortions, impressions, conditions (thoughts, emotions, beliefs, concepts, and ideas about the world, reality and the individual self). Health will only be temporary and will wane away as long as one's emotions become imbalanced again or if one is haunted by one's restless thoughts.

Q: If everything is Illusion, then why are we still here, still breathing, eating, communicating, thinking, feeling, still using money to pay bills, to buy food, clothes and to travel so that we can find inner contentment, space to 'meditate' and to attain nothingness over and over again? Would nothingness also be Illusion if everything is Maya?

A: The Natural World is a neutral illusion; it is like a platform that is given in order to experience the gradual devolution of consciousness into matter and the evolution out of it again. The way you process this illusion depends on your evolutionary level of perception and existence. If you tangle and drain yourself through every experience, then this existence becomes one of suffering for you, or shifts from suffering to experiencing temporary joy and back again. If you exist without entangling and simply live and consciously learn, then it is a pleasant existence. Both extremes, however, are temporary and should be recognised for what they truly are. Recognising this means that one has matured and evolved spiritually and understood, in their physical being through the embodiment, their true essence/actual existence, an existence that may appear for beings who are tangled with the physical matter as nothing, when in fact, it is the actual, wholesome Being.

Q: It seems as if nothingness is the actual cause for the Hell, indifference, ignorance, division, and the avoidance of responsibility in life, while the desires and the ability to live, love, feel, think, learn, forgive, experience and create a union, to grow, and to thrive for justice, equality, prosperity, freedom and a non-egocentric-based contentment are what makes nothingness disappear forever.

A: You are misinterpreting things. Your interpretation only shows all that you are now. Read the question again and see what you are. If you like what you read, then pursue your path further. You speak from the logical mind and the limited perception of reality. Your current consciousness divides reality, reacts to reality, hates and loves this reality, and all it knows is its thoughts and emotions, nothing more. But true reality is nothing for your thoughts and emotions because it is beyond it. I am not seeking to overwhelm you nor disrespect you, neither am I being sarcastic.

I understand your position, yet all you are, as you write such words, is pure emotion which has been triggered by the field/presence that is beyond your comprehension. This shows you what you are now and helps you to see your bondage. What binds you today may lead you to liberation tomorrow, provided you truly own and are responsible for what you feel right now and are conscious enough to understand it and accept it.

Q: I am really interested to know if I am comprehending you and your views or if I am projecting and misunderstanding some things and not differentiating properly.

A: You are reflecting the self; not the actual Self, but that which is limiting, binding, and causing inner struggles and fight. But this is all right, and there is no judgment in this statement, only a clear statement of that which is directly seen. Your current turmoil points to the way to being liberated from it. With time, you are going to understand this. The journey has just begun.

Q: I do not believe that life is about not helping anyone and attaining the state of nothingness.

A: True help is selfless and unconditional. Most of the time, it cannot be seen or even acknowledged because it needs no acknowledgement. True help comes from wisdom and not through the reflection of one's own miserable state of being, where you are afraid of what you see because you are afraid of being in those same shoes.

Q: I have had many questions come to my mind and heart by taking the foundational principles, philosophies and truths that were mentioned in your transmission, and I have applied them to other situations. Where do I go from here? How does one actually step on the path?

A: Current spirituality is a reflection of the collective sickness and madness of this present day and age. To truly taste Reality and that which is unconditional, one is to refine one's current perception and learn to be, and to let go of all of one's experiences and their residue. Now you experience it; now you let it go. Through misusing thoughts, emotions and memory, you bring yourself back to the past, and instead of living abundantly and contentedly now, you dwell mentally and emotionally in the past. To taste true spirituality, one needs to let go of the past on a subtle level first; this will preserve one's energy and rejuvenate one's body so that then one has enough of a capacity to simply be still so that one can eventually notice the very moment of now which is blissful and equanimous at all times. This is called true awakening to Reality. Nevertheless, it does not guarantee further evolution, because awakening means nothing without true direction and guidance and without true spiritual understanding (discernment). After awakening, people can tangle with the matter again and again and develop more superiority than before. Such beings then delude themselves and others by making a big deal out of awakening to That which is always there.

The point of spiritual evolution is inner refinement and in coming back to the Natural Being/Existence, and in understanding the essence of this illusion before dissolving it within and evolving further through subtler existence. This is Siddha knowledge. Apart from the many people who are misusing the terms Siddha, Yoga, kundalini and awakening, there are barely any publicly-known beings who have come across, tasted, or evolved through, true spiritual knowledge. This is something to ponder on.

Q: Thank you, and may good, healthy and complimenting relationships and holistic contentment be upon thee also.

A: May Siddha blessings guide you further.

EMBODYING THE TEACHING: AN ADEPT'S JOURNEY WITH JIVANMMUKTI

'At some point in our human evolution we are going to ask the simple question of how to get in touch with the real knowledge and how to come across a real teacher. How can we know who is real and who is not? These questions usually arise in the heads of those who want to know yet have not matured enough to know or to come across a genuine source of knowledge that they are able to recognise as such.

A true teaching is within each and every individual, yet to open to such a possibility within, one needs to spend a great deal of time refining the self and realising the various motives that push one into spiritual actions and ambitious pursuits. A true teaching is not a pursuit or an ambitious venture. It is a flow of the natural being and existence through the embodied being. Once one opens up to it, being mature enough mature, one is able to recognise the teaching and come across a genuine teacher.

The genuine teacher is the one who *is* the teaching and emanates this teaching through their presence in every word and action. Such a teacher's words vibrate the being, and are not just full of wisdom or familiar concepts that our minds may agree or disagree with, but are filled with the very essence of the teaching that is emanated and in whose presence each and every other being can perceive the same essence within themselves, even if only for a glimpse.

True teachers do not need to appear as bold and charismatic or as super pleasant people. In fact, such natural beings are simple and humble, and will never try to demonstrate superiority or put themselves above others in their communication with them. Yet, one may perceive subtle nobility and grace in such beings. True teachers are so called, not because they know how to teach or offer academic discourses or other types of courses, but because their entire being emanates teaching and transformation in each moment. Such beings have no desire to teach or to be in the spotlight. Such beings flow in life and do everything naturally and spontaneously. Such true gems are rare. Many people ignorantly choose to believe that some saints of the past or people who were put (by other ignorant people) on a pedestal of holiness, are truly enlightened or knowledgeable, yet for some reason they all perished and died like everyone else.

This world has not been familiar with truly enlightened beings for thousands of years, and true teachings still remain occulted from the public eye or are very hard to recognise. They will definitely not be very appealing or attractive to the majority of the current day-and-age people, because they are too subtle and too simple.

The current mind is a complex mind and looks for complexity in existence. The same applies to this current-day-and-age spirituality, which is complex and does not have true power, knowledge or transmission at its core. This is so because those who represent and teach such spirituality are not the vessels of the teaching, are not the emanations of the teaching, but rather, are entertainers, businessmen, and distorted and/or imbalanced

216

beings on various levels. Thus, they attract similar beings (the more the better) – armies of ignorant beings swamp around the most ignorant teachers.

True teachers transmit the teaching and find a response in one or two mature adepts and pass on the knowledge to them. To be able to pass on the knowledge means that these adepts are equal in potentiality to the teachers and can contain the knowledge within or, in other words, become the vessels of this knowledge too. Knowledge is like existence or space; it is always there. But in order to be able to experience it and, more-so, to contain and vibrate it, one needs to realign one's transitory being with the Ultimate one. And this is the essence of true teaching and the transmission of the Higher Being in the body.

True teachers are very rare, yet those who may contain the knowledge and to whom it can be passed on are even rarer and harder to find. Yet, no one searches. The true teacher knows who is the right vessel for the knowledge, and at the right time, activates it within the other body. It seems as if the teacher chooses the student, yet the reality is that the knowledge itself chooses the one who is eligible, mature and pure in his/her embodied being. The same knowledge-being is operating through the teacher and through the student, yet in this physical fragmented reality, it may look like one being chooses the other. No adept is able to choose the knowledge or the teacher. They may only cultivate inner purity, selflessness and trust in life. The more they are able to let go and to remain in their core, the more eligible they become for higher spheres of knowledge.

The majority of immature people find immature teachers and dead-end paths that fit their boxed-ideas of spirituality, imagination and projections, suitable to a shopper or consumer-like mentality. Such beings ignorantly believe that they may choose teachers, teachings, paths and ways/techniques to learn, and the commercial-spiritual or religious industry of today supports their notions and offers them such opportunities. Yet, no one can choose anything. In reality, such seekers are subtly manipulated into a belief that they choose, yet their choices are carefully calculated, tailored and well-marketed to them in order to match their ideas of spirituality or their current emotional/mental needs. Thus, all they choose is that which they need to choose in order to keep this corrupt spiritual and money-driven spiritual system going. The spiritual industry makes billions on people's emotional and mental traumas, psychological imbalances and victim mentality, offering them temporary solutions for which they need to pay handsomely. Yet, the plenitude of other problems remain unresolved. Similarly to our current medical system, we are offered a drug for each symptom, yet the actual root of all our diseases is kept untreated and is often even nurtured by the system, in time causing further issues for which one needs to pay again and again.

The true teaching aims at uprooting one root for all the problems, and this root is one of an ignorant existence. The true teaching offers a direct experience of the self beyond the bodily existence, and turns one's awareness to the main roots/causes of self-created and propelled misery. The true teaching leads to a massive inner awakening and sets a direction towards self-refinement. Only true self-refinement leads to the natural self-born knowledge and overall transformation on all levels. The fruit of such a transformation is the transformed and enlightened or evolved body.'

- Jivanmukti -

The experience of working with a true spiritual teacher is not something that can be boxed, pin-pointed or conceptualised in any way. A real spiritual teacher is not a static being who performs rituals, stages shows, recites pithy statements or offers temporary spiritual encouragement. Rather, the real spiritual teacher is like a condensed-in-the-body expression of the transformative and teaching force of Reality itself. A true teacher is like an eternal flow of life. It means that such a teacher assumes a unique role for each student – they emanate rather, and give only that experience to each adept which they need for their spiritual advancement/learning. Whatever these teachers give is given selflessly and automatically without any prior planning or forethought. The teacher simply lives and flows through their own being; the adept comes into that space, and through the connection that is formed therein, they begin to gradually transform and merge with the teacher's Consciousness on a subtle level. With a true teacher, every interaction can be seen as a teaching, because it is the student's/adept's higher Being that teaches them through the pure, humble-yet-powerful presence of the teacher. The presence of the teacher is the refined form through which the unconditional Being flows and expresses itself freely. And thus, such teachers do not teach. They are the teaching.

Whatever is written here is a testimonial based on my own experience of interaction with my teacher and through my own contemplation on the subject. Indeed, I can say now after many years of seeking and spiritual practice/refinement, that the pinnacle of the spiritual path is found through the acceptance of the guidance of a genuine teacher and then keeping up a consistent flow of communication, interaction and sharing with that being.

It is important to note that life itself is the fundamental spiritual teacher. We are taught through each moment in our lives, and the way our lives take shape is always perfectly designed to allow us to learn and evolve in a way that is correct and appropriate for us. The presence of the spiritual teacher in one's life is a catalysing force that seems to ignite the learning/evolutionary element in one's consciousness through the interaction with them. One may notice that the more one connects with a spiritual teacher and the path within, the more the entire flow and inner and outer trajectory of one's life begins to change and take on a qualitatively different form. Both the life circumstances and the teacher will point one to the same issues that one needs to see, refine and transform within the self.

I will now share a little about my personal experience as Jivanmukti's adept. After speaking with Jivanmukti for the first time, I instantly experienced a falling away of a certain thought and behaviour structure made up of multiple superficial and overinflated notions about myself and my direction in life. From that point on, and after committing to receive Jivanmukti's guidance and to generally position myself, as much as possible, within her space of consciousness, I have been initiated into the path of real spiritual refinement and transformation, and my whole life seems to have shifted into a mode of intense and accelerated conscious evolution, as I am somehow effortlessly pulled along by this natural current of transmission and grace. Despite doing intensive earlier practices, accumulating a lot of bookish knowledge and awareness about various teachings, living in and travelling to secluded and spiritually charged places, and gathering a tremendous amount of knowledge and experience on many subjects, I could not have possibly imagined that spiritual evolution actually happens this way or leads to such an internal breakthrough.

Making such a statement does not have any marketing or promotional value. Jivanmukti is quite a discreet being and rarely accepts anyone to learn from her directly. I consider myself fortunate, yet I also see it as a result of my own efforts to let go of all the illusions that comprised my existence earlier. This motive alone led me to this opportunity to experience true teaching in this lifetime. Yet, as I see it, my advancement always depends on me and my own ability to let go and evolve further rather than be stuck at one point or find a comfortable niche in life. And so, I was able to cultivate my being and evolve along with my teacher and not fall off so far.

To come across a true teacher does not mean, however, that one is mature enough to recognise them for who they truly are or to walk along with them. It takes time and dedication on both sides. Who the true teacher is, is not their personality but a deeply aligned and integrated nature of 'being the Ultimate in the physical form'. The form emanates that which is the Ultimate and helps true adepts recognise inner falsehood and self-destructive links with the transitory reality that drain one's physical being and energy essence.

The teacher is like a beacon of light or a reminder of the Ultimate unconditional Being. Yet, one should not foolishly imagine that a true teacher has to act within the norms of human, religious, cultural and social morality, or as one wants them to, or within the limited framework of someone else's ideas of holiness. The true teacher will destroy such hypocrisy in a blink of an eye, and strip one of all nonsense. In order to meet such a being, one has to already be free from certain constraints as well as to be aware of the ways in which falsehood and delusion manifest. It does not mean, however, that a true teacher is immoral or evil. True teachers are highly evolved in their spiritual intelligence and wisdom, which is beyond our limited human understanding. True teachers are genuinely universally moral, kind and knowledgeable, yet they are not ready to share all this with the immature beings or the beings who propel illusions within themselves. Thus, such a genuine teacher's presence alone is able to strip such delusional beings of hypocrisy, falsehood and other illusions instantly or gradually. True teachers are powerful, yet they would never demonstrate their might to the public. They are humble and joyous beings, devoid of pretension, falsehood and entanglements.

Working with Jivanmukti, I have experienced three things in particular that seem to contribute to an individual's development on this path. Firstly, there is a constant deepening sense of contentment, stillness and equanimity that runs parallel with a direct recognition of what Reality is and is not. Realising the essence of Reality as neutral, equanimous, unconditional and content being, leads one towards an indescribable inner commitment to the path, that is not based on desperation or longing, but rather, on a direct experience of what one is and what one is not. Then, one can truly commit to what is real, and gradually forego the current of what is unreal, ultimately insubstantial and evanescent.

Secondly, alongside the deepening sense of contentment, there is a rougher side: a continuous unfolding of challenges in life that push one to see the corruption within the self. For me, if I am left in a room to myself with only my own needs to worry about, I can be quite content and sit blissfully all day. But through my interaction with Jivanmukti, I have been encouraged to go down certain different avenues in life that have naturally brought up everything corrupt, distorted, victimised, fearful, selfish and narcissistic within myself – everything that I had spent my whole life unconsciously trying to hide behind, avoid or sweep under the rug. The further I go into blissful absorption and equanimity, the deeper I realise the layers of buried emotional material that arises and that I am forced to face and refine on a subtler level.

Every distorted subconscious program that originally overpowered my awareness and led to a misperception of reality and a deeper fall into illusion seems to flash back into my face through life-scenarios. These aspects naturally come to the surface to be perceived and consciously digested in a wholesome way, to be seen through the equanimous and content Being. When one refines through such a perception, one's actions and expression are also naturally transformed, as one begins to act from that being, and one's expression becomes natural, unobstructed and spontaneous; one's mind does not cling to anything and thus, one acts through freedom instead of inner contraction or stagnation. Through this process of a very intense psycho-spiritual therapy –

gradual healing and (eventually) evolution happens. The entire conditional basis of one's existence in this world is rebuilt from the position of the equanimous Being.

Thirdly, there is that spontaneous manifestation of spiritual knowledge. This knowledge seems to be a natural result of the connection between a teacher and a student/adept – Param-Para. It also seems to naturally result from the refinement process: as one perceives reality from an equanimous position, one gradually begins to see the way the reality and illusions are projected and dissolved, constructed and deconstructed. Ever since the beginning of my interaction with Jivanmukti, I feel the path, as elucidated in her book, is slowly being rewritten for me through my own being, and every day a statement or a passage from the book confirms itself within, through my own lived experience, and I am awed to say, 'Yes, it is exactly how you said it. This is the path as you have described it.'

Working with a true spiritual teacher and being connected to their presence is tough. Everywhere I try to internally hide, and whatever conditional position my mind tries to take habitually, Jivanmukti points it out to me, or it is made apparent through our interaction or through various scenarios that I face in my own daily life. Everything within me that is hypocritical, stagnant and rigid is unravelled through the presence and the invisible presence of my teacher. Even if that presence seems to be on the periphery, the direct invisible link in the space of Consciousness, does not allow any conditioning or falsehood within me to survive.

If I am living in a box, and I am acting through hypocrisy, then I will naturally impose this onto the other. And those others might not even notice or be aware of it, and apparently for the same reasons, that they themselves are on the same wavelength of falsehood and hypocrisy. Yet, with Jivanmukti, appearing totally real, lively, nothing special on the outside and very human, this is impossible. Nothing can be left unnoticed, and nothing can remain hidden in her presence. This is why, in my observation, many cannot simply face her, or they have uncontrollable fear before facing her or talking to her for the first time. I assume that they are afraid of reflecting their own limited being through that presence, or that that presence alone reminds them of their own conditionings and limitations. My experience is that she constantly escapes every box and every limited frame of reference that I naturally try to put her in through my own limited perspective, and to be honest, I am sometimes left frustrated. It is very difficult to keep up with such a being that is so absolutely fluid, direct and free-flowing in their expression. She does not act through the usual patterns of social hypocrisy, mad co-dependency and dishonesty, and thus, she exposes and reflects these aspects in the world and in the beings all around her.

To work with an evolved spiritual teacher is not predictable; rather, it is surprising, because through that interaction, instead of encountering some beautiful mystical reality, one encounters the hidden aspects of the self and the illusory fabric of hallucinatory reality that plays itself out through one's being, until one is free from this and the very beautiful and mystic reality is seen as nothing more than oneself, flowing there without any projections, separation or analysis – and the teacher and teaching are all one in that flow of self-being. Only as one begins to thin out the projected and distorted aspects does one begin to perceive the blissful and equanimous nature of reality itself.

During my time working with Jivanmukti, there have been little-to-no typical spiritualised actions, techniques or 'teachings' as the majority would imagine it. Rather, what she has consistently pointed out and revealed to me are the specific ways that distorted and unresolved issues and tendencies within my consciousness play out through my actions, expression, and general response to the world, other beings and the Reality as a whole. And by having the courage and determination to let them go, I have gradually been able to realise my own being and perceive the constant never-ending transmission of her being (teaching) – knowledge inseparable from my own. And yet, life continues, and new subtler levels of existence keep on unfolding and being refined.

I have observed spontaneous pearls of wisdom naturally and effortlessly coming from Jivanmukti through the mundane situations with adepts: her spontaneous remarks about and observations of nature, beautiful natural sceneries captured through her photography, and the teaching that flows through it silently, profound statements of spiritual wisdom and powerful life-changing (almost therapeutic) transmissions during simple conversations, through one-on-one sessions, during retreats or group interactions. I have truly realised that those transmissions that are done verbally by her and those writings and explanations are rather a low form of teaching for those who still need explanations and details about the path. They are for those who need to hold onto something to map out their journey. The higher form of teaching, however, happens through a simple connection with the presence of an evolved being that keeps on evolving and keeps on pulling the others alongside, provided those others are able to keep on refining, thinning out and letting go of the subtler and subtler constraints of the self-created and self-sustained false reality, only to embrace more and more of that vast space of unconditional existence – blissful awareness (Knowledge, Being).

I was fortunate enough to dive into the very core of the teaching beyond words and explanations. At first, however, I had to consciously dive into the very turmoil of my own torments and illusions, to eventually keep on refining, to one day emerge as a simpler, content, and more selfless being. My journey is on-going, and I daily learn about life through my own and other beings.

I have never had any sense that Jivanmukti thinks that she is a teacher or is anyhow special, different, 'enlightened' or 'spiritual'. Rather, I see that there is no thought of being anything in particular, but there is just Being itself in absolute simplicity, purity, freedom of expression and radical honesty to the self and others. I cannot say that Jivanmukti is this or that Jivanmukti is that. Even if I were to say that Jivanmukti is purity – then what is purity? When we use words, we create notions and have our own ideas of what things mean. Yet, true being is beyond words and words then, would only be a means to box something that is free at its essence, in its core. It is just Beingness itself.

When I contemplate on Jivanmukti's essence, I am immediately returned to that Space within the self. Through her mirror, I see both my own and the collective's distortions, hypocrisies and limitations; through perceiving her essence, I perceive the Ultimate Being that is beyond form, time or any conceptualisation, and is forever blissful and supreme in every sense. This is how I have come to perceive, and this is why I call Jivanmukti my Guru and Being. For the rest of the world, she appears as an absolutely ordinary being, devoid of anything special or extraordinary; simple, friendly, joyful like a child, with a peculiar sense of humour, witty and hard to grasp sometimes, friendly yet very straightforward and sharp, direct and honest, extremely concentrated when engaged in certain activities, and very fluid, deeply aware of various aspects of life and highly knowledgeable about various aspects of existence, extremely selfless and very strict with selfish beings, generous and sharing, absorbed and silent.

Being in touch with Jivanmukti, I have discovered multiple sides of her supposed personality, yet with time, I realised that these are facets of life that manifest through her being and reflect or adjust to the beings of those she interacts with. Thus, there is such a range of qualities that are only reflections that manifest through that blissful equanimous emptiness and thus, are hard to describe and put into one limited personality framework. Jivanmukti's qualities of selflessness, child-like simplicity and pure self-expression are among those that showed me the true subtle and hard-to-notice-for-the-majority direction in my spiritual journey, the pillars of her true personality that are always there and that made me realise the essence of her earthly being. For me, this utter simplicity in this corrupt day and age is already unique and hard to find. I am genuinely grateful within myself to have been able to come across and learn through Jivanmukti's presence.

ABOUT JIVANMUKTI

Jivanmukti is the vessel of Siddha Param-Para, and a stream of living transmission, self-born knowledge and spontaneous teaching. Jivanmukti's words carry in them an immense spiritual power to return one to the natural flow of life, to invoke the living spiritual teaching within and to dispel illusions on the path of awakening and self-refinement. Jivanmukti's presence is that of a pure selfless and often-unpredictable (for the logical mind) being, the being that is conscious, free and unconditional in self-expression, the being that represents the very flow of life, teaching and learning, and multiple possibilities/ways to evolve in and beyond the world of names and forms.

www.siddhakundaliniyoga.com

www.siddhantayoga.com

SIDDHANTA YOGA PUBLICATIONS

Available exclusively at
www.siddhakundaliniyoga.com

SIDDHA PARAM-PARA
The Original I-VI Parts - Collector's Edition

Available on Amazon

New Edition of Siddha Param-Para (Parts I-VII)

Reviving the Original Yoga Sutras: The Secret Teachings of Siddha Patanjali

Printed in Great Britain
by Amazon

29429669R00141